About the

Harriet Kelsall is one of the most respected bespoke designers and creative business trailblazers working in the UK jewellery industry today. She was the 2016 HSBC Forward Ladies 'National Retail Business Woman of the Year', Everywoman's 'Retail Woman of the Year' in 2011, one of the *IoD Director* magazine's six 'Women who have most changed the business world' in 2014 and is a Freeman of the Worshipful Company of Goldsmiths of the City of London.

Originally taught to make jewellery by her father who was a keen and talented hobby jeweller, Harriet always had a passion for goldsmithing and made her first silver ring with him at the age of four. She founded her business – Harriet Kelsall Bespoke Jewellery – in 1998 at her kitchen table.

As a passionate advocate for skills and education within her sector, Harriet helps the Government as a jewellery industry adviser for the Creative and Cultural Skills Academy. She is the Chairman of the National Association of Jewellers as well as a non-executive director at both the Responsible Jewellery Council and the British Hallmarking Council. She is 'Master' to an apprentice from the Worshipful Company of Goldsmiths, and can often be found speaking to inspire other creatives. She was a 'Titan of Industry' with Doug Richard's School for Creative Startups, and also for the Peter Jones Academy in Hertfordshire, mentoring students and small business directors.

As a champion for ethics, in 2011 she helped launch Fairtrade gold worldwide and her business became the first in the world to be both Fairtrade licensed and certified by the Responsible Jewellery Council.

Other Titles

The Creative's Guide to Starting a Business

Harriet Kelsall

ROBINSON

ROBINSON

First published in Great Britain in 2018
by Robinson

10 9 8 7 6 5 4 3 2 1

A CIP catalogue record for this book
is available from the British Library.

ISBN: 978-1-47214-109-5

Typeset in Sentinel by SX Composing DTP,
Rayleigh, Essex
Printed and bound in Great Britain by CPI
Group (UK), Croydon CR0 4YY

Papers used by Robinson are from well-
managed forests and other responsible
sources.

MIX
Paper from
responsible sources
FSC® C104740
www.fsc.org

Robinson
An imprint of
Little, Brown Book Group
Carmelite House
50 Victoria Embankment
London EC4Y 0DZ

An Hachette UK Company
www.hachette.co.uk

www.littlebrown.co.uk

How To Books are published by
Robinson, an imprint of Little, Brown
Book Group. We welcome proposals
from authors who have first-hand
experience of their subjects.
Please set out the aims of your book,
its target market and its suggested
contents in an email to
Nikki.Read@howtobooks.co.uk.

Contents

Foreword

In a world that faces great global challenges, entrepreneurship is increasingly seen as the powerful vehicle that will enable us to deliver solutions to these challenges. Why is that? Because entrepreneurs see the world differently, not only as it is but how it could be, and then find a way to make the world they see real. Isn't that very similar to creatives? Entrepreneurs and creatives see a different world and bring it to life through their creations. Entrepreneurship is also in itself an inherently creative process that I will discuss in a little more detail below, but before I go into that, I'd like to emphasise the role that creatives and entrepreneurs play in delivering to us a new world. Put simply, we cannot hope for a better future if we don't change the behaviours and systems that are getting us into trouble, such as overpopulation, lack of nutritious food, consumerism, pollution, climate change, inequality, biodiversity loss, etc. Maintaining the system is 'management'; changing the system is 'entrepreneurship'.

Entrepreneurship is about having a vision, and going about making it real without being held back by what you have, or can do, right now. I'm broadly paraphrasing the following Harvard Business School definition of entrepreneurship that was coined by Professor Howard Stevenson in 1995: '*entrepreneurship* is the pursuit of opportunity beyond resources controlled'. This implies a drive to create something that is needed (opportunity), probably something new (if it is already available, then it is unlikely to be an opportunity), working around/through certain constraints (beyond resources controlled) and making it happen anyway.

To create and find ways to make things work is a creative process, and an entrepreneur needs to be creative at pretty much every step of their journey. Turning a creative passion into a business is therefore a creative endeavour in and of itself, well beyond the ideation or product design stages. You will have noticed that this definition does not include anything about making money. That's because entrepreneurship in not focused on making money but on making things happen, creating value. Making money comes in when you want to set up and run a successful business. That's the definition of business: providing goods or services that you get paid for.

This book describes the processes and choices that will face any entrepreneur, highlights the natural affinity between creatives and entrepreneurship and shares some down-to-earth practical guidance on how to build a business around making new and wonderful, beautiful things that people want to buy. Don't underestimate the wisdom that Harriet provides because of this book's accessibility. She provides sound principles and good advice via a personal and very approachable narrative. She covers complex theories and concepts such as effectuation, social capital, self-efficacy, reflexive practice and more, without ever using a single pompous word. Harriet leaves that to us academics who study what people like her do and give these theories and concepts awkward names that make us sound smart, or at least deter people from asking us any difficult questions (you can't ask a question if you don't know what we're talking about). I assure you it is very effective!

More seriously, Harriet has managed in one book to offer inspiration and practical support for what you need to do to set up a business around a creative endeavour. She guides the creative entrepreneur with stories and a structure towards understanding yourself, developing an entrepreneurial mindset, being prepared for success (most people spend their time worrying about 'what if it all goes wrong'; what if it all goes spectacularly well?), how to play to your strengths and how to complement them, how to think about what you do and adjust when you need to, how and why to be flexible, and most importantly to value and embrace continuous learning. In my opinion the three key strengths of this book are:

1. It's clear, simple and practical: no unnecessary complications, just sound business advice from a well-informed, experienced, successful creative entrepreneur who has helped many others build successful businesses. This will help you build your confidence as well as your business, and these are equally important. Your confidence is a self-fulfilling prophecy: if you think you can, you probably will be able to, and if you think you cannot, you will not.

2. It busts the myth that there is a particular type of person or set of characteristics that is unique to entrepreneurs. In fact, there is no single profile or set of characteristics that is shared by all successful entrepreneurs. Some may share behaviour traits, but not always. However, there is a shared mindset that is illustrated in the cases throughout the book.

3. The structure and practical exercises allow you to build the pieces of the business as you go through, and then to pull it all together when you are ready. It is tempting to read the exercise, conclude that you get it, and move on. Of course you get it; after all, it is not rocket science. However, make the effort to articulate what you are asked to do. It makes all the difference. Once you have to commit to the actual words, it becomes clear where some of your thinking might still need to be developed.

It is important to keep in mind that you don't have to do it alone – you have people around you to guide and support you, and you will meet many more along the way. People on the whole are happy to help, so do ask for assistance when you know what you need. This book will get you a long way, but is not a substitute for talking to others, drawing inspiration from them, and reaching out to mentors as and when you need them. That's called social capital.

With this book you will be able clarify your destination as well as the steps and direction you need to take to move towards that destination. It ultimately does not matter if you meander a little (even a lot in some cases); as long as you are moving in the right direction you're still making progress. Your ideas and outcomes will change along the way – that's a fact of business and entrepreneurship. It's normal and it's healthy. This book will help you give life to a business that is authentic to you as you travel through your entrepreneurial journey. Harriet is open and generous with sharing her experience, and her book is about realising your dream(s) and making money along the way. Her warmth and love for the creative industries, entrepreneurship and helping others comes through on every page. I wish you all the same enjoyment I had reading this book and its stories of such diverse, creative entrepreneurs and, above all, I wish you a very successful realisation of your new business.

Dr Shima Barakat, MBA
Entrepreneurship Education Advisor
University of Cambridge Office of Postdoctoral Affairs

Preface

This book is for anybody who has creative talent that they want to use to make products that they feel can sell. This might be fashion, ceramics, cushions, hats, jewellery, sculptures, cards, flower arrangements, paintings, sugar-craft, upholstery . . . just anything beautiful.

If your creativity is much more to you than just a pastime and you are producing beautiful things of a professional quality, perhaps you have wondered what it would take to turn their production into your career. Might you be able to branch into a whole new direction? Might you be able to give up your less interesting 'day job' and start a business?

Perhaps you get a lot of compliments about your work and are already seeing a demand. Perhaps you have been selling some of your pieces online or at exhibitions. Have friends begun to ask you to make products for them?

If you are wondering what it would take to move your creative products to a different level and start a business, this book will tell you how to make that step and help you to decide whether this move is something that you want to work towards.

Today, we are surrounded by many platforms and tools to help and support creative entrepreneurs, such as Pinterest, YouTube, Facebook, Instagram, Not On The High Street and even Etsy or eBay. Every year, creatives can find a myriad of new routes to customers. Creative people are naturally brilliant at thinking of different ways to approach their market. There has never been a better time to begin to turn your creative passion into your career.

Can Anyone Start a Business?

The answer to this question is yes; anybody can start a business and it isn't really very difficult. This chapter explores which qualities are common in successful creative founders and illustrates these with interesting stories and case studies.

Twenty years ago, I certainly didn't set out to 'start a business' and I didn't know what an 'entrepreneur' was back then; I set out to create beautiful individual jewellery and somewhere along the way I looked back and noticed that I had started a business as part of that journey. I wish I had better understood everything that I have written down in this book when I started out because it would have enabled me to start more confidently and perhaps to have achieved creative and financial success more easily.

As a creative person, you'll generally have a huge passion and drive to make things with your hands – to design, create and innovate. At some point, this can steer you towards trying to sell your pieces and then, by default, you'll need to start a business to facilitate this. If you are driven by a real passion to make your creative business succeed, you will find it relatively easy to spend lots of time on your work, figure out new and innovative solutions to any problems that come your way and be passionate about making sure that your products are desired by your customers.

You don't have to have a business qualification, be good at maths or a computer whizz to start a business. You don't have to spend five hours a day on social media to build a successful start-up. You don't need any

A-levels. You certainly don't need to be anything like those characters on reality TV shows like *The Apprentice*. I started a successful and innovative creative business, and so can you.

What qualities make a successful creative entrepreneur?

You do have to be prepared to work hard and work to your market, but creating a successful start-up really is within your reach. While anybody can start a business, there are eight qualities that I have noticed in many (but not all) successful start-up founders:

1. Drive to succeed

Your potential as a creative entrepreneur is not only about your talent as an artist but also about your drive and determination to succeed. I can think of a number of examples of mediocre creatives who have succeeded despite their questionable talents because they have a huge drive and work like crazy. However, I can't think of any examples of highly talented creatives who have managed to succeed despite lacking drive and not putting in the hours. So it could even be argued that the determination to succeed is even more important than your talent!

Another aspect of this same point is that successful creatives are people who can finish what they start. They need to be able to finish each piece of work that they produce and also each different task they have to fulfil along the path to making their work a success.

Celia Persephone Gregory, a mosaic artist, sculptor and marine conservationist, explains that the ability to finish what she starts is part of what helps her to be a successful entrepreneur.

Many people undertake a big creative project but don't ever manage to actually finish it. 'I just have to complete what I start and do not feel fulfilled until I have done so. Perhaps it is because I always want my work to have an audience and, of course, this never happens until it is complete.'

Celia has been able to connect marine conservation, her art and sculpture in an entirely innovative way by being completely focused on completion and never giving up; this drive has helped her overcome many problems along the way. 'Ideas are cheap when you are creative – but no idea becomes realised until you actually do it. You have to face the problems realising them in the real world – whether that is overcoming structural issues as you build it or working out how you write or form it. As you produce your idea, things will always pop up and you have to solve the real world problems. An idea doesn't bring to you all of the realities of making it happen.'

A successful entrepreneur will stop at nothing to overcome or alter these problems until they realise their creative business vision.

2. Seize opportunities

Personally, I am a great believer in making the most of the opportunities you have been handed. When I went to a friend's wedding and gem-buying trip to Sri Lanka twenty years ago, the poorer street children there used to beg for pens or pencils. They couldn't afford them but were desperate to learn to write in order to pull themselves out of their situation. I chatted with young adults there who simply wanted me to spare ten minutes of my time so that they could practise their English, realising that improved language skills might open up a job opportunity for them in tourism. It was an eye-opener compared with many of our kids here in the UK who are handed everything on a plate and still often don't grasp their potential.

Unfortunately, not everybody is given the same opportunities in life. Nobody's life feels easy to them but if you have been able to go to school and earned some qualifications or have learned a creative skill, then you are very lucky. If you have managed both, then you are even better off. Please don't take these gifts for granted, but make the most of them. Starting a business is a brilliant way to make the most of your skills, combining elements from all different areas of your life.

When you run a business, opportunities will come your way and you need to be able to think creatively about them and be willing to seize the ones that are right for you and reject the ones that are not. Sometimes you can turn problems or odd situations into learning opportunities. Sometimes it is about changing your mindset; instead of thinking of a difficult situation as annoying and whingeing that somebody else should come and fix it, imagine what you might learn from tackling it and visualise how you will use that experience in your future business.

I had my own very steep learning curve when I seized an opportunity that was presented to me when still only a teenager. I ended up running a restaurant with no experience, but learned a lot, and it helped to grow my entrepreneurial potential.

One summer when we were seventeen, my friend Marianne and I decided to look for some waitressing work despite having no previous experience. As we entered one pub, a lady rushed past us and it turned out that this was the restaurant manager storming out! The owners had their heads in their hands and we could not have arrived at a better time. We slightly exaggerated our capabilities, saying, 'We have a lot of experience in pubs,' which wasn't exactly a lie. Before we knew it, we had been asked to run the entire restaurant for three weeks while the owners went on holiday.

The owners departed the next day and, amazingly, left the restaurant entirely in our hands, telling us that a couple would be arriving from Australia the following day, having been recruited on a working holiday; these would be our staff.

We had only eaten in restaurants a handful of times and knew almost nothing. The chef refused to speak to us for several days and did everything he could to disrupt everything. He would purposefully heat plates up so they couldn't be touched and say we had to take them out without gloves and then shout at us for disobeying him. I told him that I would have to get hold of the owner and disturb their holiday if he kept putting us in danger. The nasty tricks stopped but the shouting didn't.

The first evening, we made sure we arrived early as we didn't think that the cutlery and glasses looked very clean and we wanted to take a little time to sort this out. I'd never pulled a pint before and, after many experimental glasses of froth, we decided to delegate serving the drinks to the Australian couple.

Luckily for us, the restaurant was fairly quiet on that first Saturday night and we only had something like ten covers to handle. We somehow managed to learn as we went along and got through it OK.

In the time we were there, we also had to organise a couple of functions that had been booked into the restaurant. Marianne accidentally tripped, showering a charity gathering with whitebait. They weren't best pleased, but we managed to keep upbeat (actually trying not to giggle at how seriously they took themselves while surrounded by small fried fish). We gave them an extra bottle of wine and soon had them smiling again and enjoying their function.

We worked really hard but thoroughly enjoyed it. Towards the end of our third week, the restaurant manager returned. I think she thought that the restaurant couldn't run without her, but she was wrong.

Hopefully, she had learned, as I did, that nobody should be indispensable in a well-run business.

We'd established quite a nice little team with the Australian couple and even the chef had stopped shouting. We had new regulars and the restaurant was a lot busier than it had been when we started. In some ways, we were sad to leave that little community behind, but it was time to concentrate on our A-levels.

The lessons I learned in such a short time have been invaluable to me while running my business. I learned about managing people who were older than me and sometimes tricky to deal with. I also discovered that simple, low-cost improvements to the customer experience can make a huge difference to how much money you earn; and that throwing somebody in at the deep end can work as long as they care.

There is nothing like undertaking new experiences, especially if they take you right out of your comfort zone. If you already know that you need to improve your confidence, then waiting on tables or a retail job can be hugely beneficial.

3. Putting in the hours

To get your business up and running, you will be working all hours at first, often including weekends. The good news is that during much of this time, you are doing something that you absolutely love, so many of the hours you spend really don't feel at all like hard work!

I have spoken to many individuals who cite that the main reason that they want to start a business is because they want to improve their lifestyle or to spend more time with their family. It is certainly true that being your own boss means that you can be more flexible about your working hours. However, wanting more time off or an easier life are not usually reliable reasons to start a business, because this is not what starting a business will usually give you (at least not at first). When you start your own company, your lifestyle can be more challenging for a little while in some ways. If you have rent to pay and food to buy, you won't be able to afford much time off for the first year or two. You don't get holiday pay and neither can you claim sick pay if you are ill. This also means, by the way, that you might want to consider a simple health insurance policy further down the line.

4. Enjoying variety

When you run a business, you will need to spend some time each week on things which are not your creative passion. For example, you will have to start becoming quite disciplined about saving receipts and carefully recording what you spend and charge, and you will need to take time updating your website or calling people trying to get the word about your creations 'out there'.

The everyday job of the owner of a start-up is very varied. Personally, this suits me really well because I like variety in my working day and get bored easily.

5. Self-motivation

If you are the sort of person who struggles to find the energy to go and do a few hours of extra work at the weekend then it is good to remember that you won't have a boss telling you what to do, but the work still needs to be done. You'll ideally need to be the sort of person who can find a way to push through (sometimes even enjoy) the boring jobs as well as the fun, creative stuff. I think of these jobs as necessary to complete in order to get on with the things I really love.

I have noticed that many successful entrepreneurs are the sort of people who have trouble stopping work at the end of the day and are not usually people who have trouble motivating themselves to start work.

Another thing about starting a business is that it can feel a bit lonely at times. At first, you are likely to be working on your own a lot and this can feel isolating. It is worth thinking about how you will combat this and who you will talk to each day. For example, perhaps you can join a local creative hub or some other kind of unrelated class each week that gets you out of the house and engaging with like-minded individuals. With this kind of contact, you will not feel at all lonely and, in fact, will hopefully feel even more inspired and excited by your work.

6. Creative learning

I think another important quality for the owner of a start-up is the ability and enthusiasm to learn in unconventional ways. It is great to use your creativity to learn things on a shoestring.

It is quite fun to spend some of your spare time improving your prospects on your own; after all, it is for your benefit. Teaching yourself new skills probably comes fairly naturally to you in your creative world, so harness that and apply it to other areas, too. For example, you might need to focus on learning things like a bit of marketing or social networking in the same way.

You don't usually have to go on a training course to learn something new and actually you won't always be able to afford this anyway. If I hadn't taught myself the advanced jewellery-making skills that I needed or read a text on bookkeeping in my spare time, I wouldn't be writing this book now.

There are hundreds of other ways to learn on your own and they are cheaper and often better than attending a training course: read; surf the Internet; look on YouTube; do an online course; or find a relevant group on a meeting-up app.

It is a good idea to think of different ways to find out what you need. Ask friends with relevant skills for basic one-to-one training courses in return for you doing something else for them. For example, you could make something for them or take their kids out for an afternoon. Or you could volunteer to help organise something relevant on a charity committee in your spare time. This is a good way to begin growing your skill base and your network with your future start-up ambitions in mind.

7. Flexibility

Successful creatives often have to be prepared to change. For example, if you produce a collection of your work that the market does not like or cannot afford, you need to be prepared to learn from this and change your offerings to appeal more effectively to your market – more on that later. So it is important for you to consider how you might be willing to adapt your products or services if necessary.

8. Collaboration

Just being nice to everybody is a great place to start! Even if you are the sole director of your business, it is great to be collaborative. It is good to try to meet other start-up owners, too. If you can work with other people in lots of different ways, share skills and help each other out, this will get you all off to a better start.

There will be times over the long term where you will appreciate having somebody to lean on and I think that taking on a business partner a few years ago has helped me significantly. With the right partner, you have two full-time drivers of your business, which can be fantastic. However, it can also be a huge challenge if the two partners have different visions, don't feel they are pulling an equal load or if they fall out, so choose carefully.

What if you don't have all the qualities needed?

Please remember that the above eight points are just something that I have noticed in many (but not all) successful creative business founders. If you don't have all of the traits listed above, please don't be put off, as I don't think very many entrepreneurs have every single one of those! There are lots of exceptions, some of whom have contributed the case studies in this book.

There are so many positive things about running your own business. There are far too many to list here, but they include the fact that you can do things exactly how you want them done, you can set up your environment and working week so that it is perfect for you, and you can reap the numerous rewards and recognition as a successful creative entrepreneur.

Setting up with a partner

One thing worth considering before you start is setting up your business with somebody else. Obviously, you can only consider this if you have somebody who wants to go into business with you and who balances your skills and who you can trust and get along well with.

I didn't really consider partnership when I started out, but I think maybe I should have done. If I hadn't had my husband Tim, who has become a strong business partner for at least the last few years and a sounding board for much longer, the business would not be doing as well as it is today. Tim handles a lot of the processes and operations of the business, while I direct creativity and technical jewellery knowledge and standards. We both combine our different viewpoints successfully with the marketing, PR and other areas of the business.

Sometimes, businesses start in this way right from the outset, but often a partner comes on board a little later which is what happened with Keith, a renowned ceramicist, and Dominic:

Case Study

MAKE International is a provider of contemporary homeware, in which Keith Brymer Jones is the creative driver while Dominic Speelman controls the finances. Dominic persuaded Keith into partnership, which enabled Keith to grow his brand and embrace mass production.

As a sole trader, Keith did well and his work was soon picked up by retailers. Several years on, he was still hand-making everything himself throwing as many as 1,000 pots in a single day. In 2008, he was at a trade show when he met Dominic Speelman, who had spent a few years living in China sourcing homeware products for European companies. Dominic wanted to get into ceramics manufacture and had loads of contacts but no design flair. Keith warmed to Dominic straight away and liked his frank and honest manner. Dominic loved Keith's work and explained that he could get it mass-produced, suggesting, 'I have no idea about design and am even colour blind, so how about you do the pots and I'll do the pennies?'

Keith was a bit sceptical about the idea of manufacturing in factories at first, worrying about the quality. He confesses having wondered, 'What does this toff know?' but when Dominic brought back a sample piece of one of Keith's designs from China, he was amazed and impressed by the quality. Two weeks later, they were on a plane to China together to look at the factories . . . and so their partnership began.

The two collaborators hit it off straight away and, for a long time, their business relationship was held together only by trust. It is certainly true that trust is one of the most important factors of any partnership, but it is wise to get a formal partnership contract drawn up early on.

As a result of Keith and Dominic's successful partnership, MAKE International now offers fantastic opportunities to fresh new designers, which is something that Keith particularly enjoys. 'I get very emotional when I think about giving people like me that kind of chance,' he says, 'and it is so moving to see their faces when they open up their first royalty cheque.'

Working with a partner can also be an effective solution when you know you lack skills and need to find a way to get them into your business but can't afford to employ somebody, and this is what Anna Scholz found worked really well for her business:

Case Study

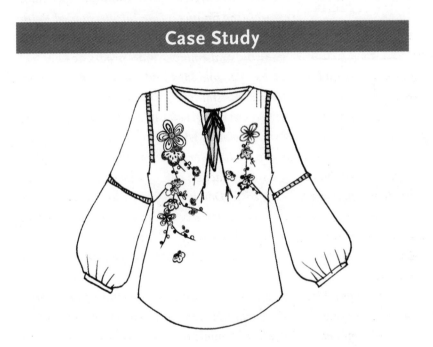

At Anna Scholz, Exclusively Plus Size Fashion, Cliff started off as Anna's friend and adviser but they ended up forming a partnership which Anna achieved by offering him a percentage of the business.

Like Keith and Dominic, Anna and Cliff have clearly defined roles, which means that they don't step on each other's toes. Anna was in her mid-twenties when she started her business and knew that she found numbers boring but that they were important; she realised that she needed Cliff's experience and financial knowledge but had nothing to pay him. So she offered him a percentage of the business; of course, at first this was a percentage of nothing. However, he believed in Anna and the brand's potential and found it interesting and challenging as it was so different from his usual work.

Creative people often get enthusiastic when they see materials that they can use to make beautiful things and Anna confesses that, left to her own devices, she might fall in love with a great fabric which is really too expensive. So Cliff ensures that the figures always make sense. Anna advises, 'It is important to be commercially driven as well as creative and aspirational, so a good accountant or financial adviser is very important.'

Successful partnerships involving two creatives are rarer. Sometimes, though, they can be both brilliant and emotionally turbulent – John Lennon and Paul McCartney; Andy Warhol and Jean-Michel Basquiat; and F. Scott Fitzgerald and Zelda, to name but a few. However, they can work wonderfully well when the two have a united vision. Frances and Dominic at Scabetti have just such a partnership:

Case Study

Sometimes partnerships can work well with a successful creative overlap and joint vision as is shown in this case study from Dominic and Frances Bromley of Scabetti, an art and design studio creating contemporary ceramic lighting, art installations and tableware.

After twelve years working together full time, Frances and Dominic both now feel that they couldn't work alone quite as well, and that they complement each other perfectly. They come up with their ideas and develop their concepts together. They are equally talented, degree-qualified industrial designers with completely different approaches and skills. Dominic focuses on the integrity of the pieces and is very contemplative, keeping strong visual control over the way they are presented in every image or piece of printed material. Frances is a positive thinker and creative problem-solver, who understands the market and their brand appeal.

They manage to find ways to split creative tasks very effectively. For example, they recently made a piece that comprises many male and female forms. After developing the idea together for an exhibition in Limoges, Frances sculpted the male form and Dominic sculpted the female form. They then combined their skills to turn this exhibition idea into a successful product called 'Ascension'.

The couple have different approaches and motivations but always agree on what feels right and what is beautiful. Like all good partnerships, they seem to achieve even more together than their individual talents might have accomplished separately.

However your idea for a partnership forms and evolves, it is advisable to have clearly defined roles. Just as we've seen in previous case studies, this might be where someone takes care of the creative direction and the other the finance and operations. Or perhaps the responsibility for each project is discussed and roles are adapted, so that where one creative input ends and the other begins is understood by both partners.

I have included interactive exercises throughout this book to encourage you to think more deeply about yourself, your creativity and your business aspirations. Many of these exercises have been helpful to the creatives I have mentored and I hope that you will enjoy them, too. Some of them ask the questions that will already be on your mind, while others will encourage you to look at things from a different perspective.

While it can still be helpful to go through these verbally, I would encourage you to take the time to write down the answers carefully in a dedicated notebook as you will want to refer back to them later. If you complete all of my exercises throughout the book, you will find that most of your written answers will give you a head start when writing your business plan in Chapter 12.

Exercise 1

1. Write down 10 reasons why you want to start a business.

2. Now summarise the most important ones into a single sentence to answer the question: 'Why do I want to start a business?'

Exercise 2

Score the following questions 0-10 with 0 being 'No way!' and 10 being 'Yes - absolutely!':

1. How would you feel about working a seven-day week for one entire month?

2. Have you ever, or would you consider teaching yourself a completely new skill from scratch in your own time?

3. How would you feel about buying yourself a book or heavily researching online to learn a skill you don't have (e.g. basic bookkeeping or designing a website) and teaching yourself this skill?

4. Do you think that you are self-motivated?

5. Do your parents/family/closest friends also believe you are self-motivated? Ask five of them to score you here to find an average score.

6. Would you be prepared to change or adapt your designs/products to make them more attractive to your customers?

7. How do you feel about potentially spending a whole week without seeing anybody else during your working hours?

8. Have you already sold any of your pieces?

9. How would you feel about spending a whole day typing everything that you have spent this month into your computer and filing it all neatly?

10. If you submitted ten of your most time-consuming pieces to a shop/exhibition and none of them sold, how would you feel about completely reworking or rethinking them?

Scoring

Add up your points, and if you scored 70 or more you probably already have all it takes to start a business; with 30-70 points, you may have a few things to work on before you start. If you scored 30 or less, then you might want to think very hard about these factors before going further down the business start-up route.

2

When Is the Best Time to Start a Business?

You can start a successful creative business at any time. There are examples of successful creative businesses started at all different stages of life. I've met people who started up while still at school, after redundancy, during retirement, before and after maternity leave or after the kids have grown and left home. Others, like me, decided to change career direction, or perhaps drastic life changes revealed a new and surprising time to start up. This chapter explores when might be the *ideal* time to start a business.

Being financially independent

You don't want to be in a position where you need financial support from anyone, such as a partner or parents, for more than six months. If you become used to relying on someone else to pay the bills, you risk becoming an unrealistic and unsustainable business person.

Understanding the working world before launching your own business

It is not ideal to start a business straight out of education. It is much better to understand what the working world is like first and gain a bit of life experience by working in different companies and industries first. There are, of course, some people who have managed brilliant creative start-ups straight from art college, but this is rare and, generally, the more experience you have before you start, the better your business will be.

Steve Shipman of Steve Shipman Wedding Photography advises that it is best not to start a business straight after college or university.

Steve felt lucky when he left college because he managed to get a job as a photography assistant. He suggests that it is best for students or new graduates to get some creative business experience with somebody else first, if possible, saying, 'The experience you get doesn't have to be in the same field that you are passionate about; go somewhere where you can learn how to cost things up and how to make a profit without being greedy. You need to observe and learn how people find the market that they want to work for and then how they pitch themselves to that market.'

Steve is a great believer in learning about the history of your creative field, advising, 'I think you need to know about whose shoulders you are standing on and why . . . you need a real understanding of where they are coming from.'

This is something that you can easily do by working for established creatives and also by visiting galleries, browsing online and reading books while you build your business idea.

Gaining as many of the skills you need before you start

Even if you are an expert in your particular creative passion, there are still a lot of business skills you'll need to learn, such as bookkeeping, how to produce business cards, and even how to create your own website. Make a list of everything that you think you need to learn and, if possible, show it to somebody who already runs their own business to fill in any gaps. Then you can plan and schedule how and what to learn.

Starting your business while still employed

Don't feel you have to stop full-time employment before you start taking steps towards setting up your own business. As you will see later on in this chapter, I ran a small version of my business at home for friends-of-friends in my spare time for quite a while before I quit my day job. You can do loads of research, try a few things out and even begin to build up a portfolio of commissions so you get established before you actually decide you can stop your regular pay cheque. Your boss might tolerate your moving to part-time hours for a while, too.

Being ready to take the plunge

The day will come when you do push beyond your comfort zone and stick your neck out to succeed. There are ways you can minimise the risk but, if you don't try it, you'll never know. Remember that every founder makes mistakes regularly and you'll usually learn more from your mistakes than your successes.

Getting things off the ground before or after having children

Whatever your gender, if you do plan to have kids, it is a good idea to have your business off the ground comfortably before you start a family if you can; children are pretty all-consuming when they are little.

Personally, I found it very hard to have kids while running the business – this is a fine juggling act, but it is possible. So don't despair if you are reading this and the timing just doesn't seem ideal. You will find a way of making it work if you really want to.

If you are a woman who might want to give birth in the future, you need to be able to leave your business for at least two weeks to have a child. This is the minimum leave allowed by maternity law and your body needs to recover. Whether you are the mother or the father, you will want to take some leave, but you can't abandon your business for too long or you will lose touch and it may fall apart. So have a think about this well in advance and be sure to have a support plan in place.

Some great businesses are started by parents who take maternity or childcare as an opportunity to completely change their life and start a business. Here are two entirely different examples:

Case Study

Dominic and Frances Bromley of Scabetti got their ceramic lighting, installations and tableware business off the ground while juggling childcare. The initial years of Scabetti had to fit around their family priorities.

Dominic and Frances had their first child, Hannah, as Dominic graduated from university, where they had both gained degrees in industrial design. Initially, Dominic stayed at home looking after her, while Frances took a great job at the toymaker, Hasbro. After a year being a stay-at-home dad, Dominic took on a full-time job at a design consultancy.

When Hannah started school a few years later, they felt one of them should be there to collect her each day. Frances was offered a great promotion at Hasbro, so she once again became the sole breadwinner and Dominic gave up his job to fit around their family priorities. But Dominic took this time as an opportunity to focus on starting a business. Because of Frances' salary, they didn't financially need to make the business work straight away so Dominic took time to explore his creativity and see if he could find a market at the end of his journey.

Frances joined the company full-time nearly fifteen years ago and they went on to build on the initial success together. They now have beautiful, high-profile installations across the world and are successful and extremely well respected.

When I asked if they think it's a good idea for somebody to start a business straight after university, Frances said, 'Put it this way, we have a twenty-four-year-old daughter and she won't work with us until she has experience in the real world.' They both see their previous work experience as vital in shaping them as professional designers and as individuals who appreciate how lucky they are to be working for themselves. Both think it is better to experience other things before starting a business. They also feel that having been employees themselves in the past means that they understand what staff need and expect; this helps them with their own team now.

Case Study

Nanna Sandom, founder of Splendid Stitches, a business specialising in vintage clothing alterations and repairs, reassessed her working life after becoming the mother of two.

When Nanna had her first child, she realised her life working as a successful brand manager in a publishing company was not compatible with her changed lifestyle. She suddenly realised that she wasn't doing what she wanted with her life and that the frantic pace of her old job didn't really allow her the 'head space' to see that she actually wanted to start a creative business. She wanted to fulfil a lifelong passion for dressmaking, which had started when she was growing up in Denmark.

Nanna managed to work part-time while starting the business and is now in her fourth successful business year. After the birth of her second child, she left her publishing job and went full-time with her own alteration business. She doesn't wish that she had started her business before having her children because she has found her corporate experience so useful and recognises that she would not have been capable of starting a business before having become a mother as being on maternity leave helped her realise what she wanted. Being a mum means that she has to take more time over each stage, so she works a 12–15-hour week and she has a year-by-year plan to grow her business slowly but surely. Working part-time doesn't make her any less energetic or ambitious but it slows down the business growth to a more manageable pace.

Starting a business after a life-changing event

Sometimes, significant life changes can result in an attitude shift which leads to starting a business. For example, many successful businesses have started after redundancy, relocation, bereavement or a forced change in circumstances. These kinds of life changes are, of course, extremely difficult to deal with, but focusing on your creativity can perhaps help you get through these challenging times and the unexpected can sometimes present surprising opportunities.

Laura Sparling is a designer whose lampwork beads company was founded by Laura after the death of her mother.

Since 2004, Laura had been growing her passion for creating hand-made lampwork glass beads while still working full-time. She gradually set up a workbench in her garden shed and began selling her beads on eBay.

Laura and her mum ran their print-finishing business from home and it provided them with a very good income. When her mum died in 2006, Laura decided that she couldn't bear to carry on the family business without her. It was suddenly the perfect time to throw herself into starting a successful bead-making business. She had some savings and was still living at home with her dad so she had enough to live on for a while. She remembers thinking that she'd give it six months and, after that, if she was managing to make enough money to survive, she'd carry on.

She says that even though she probably still doesn't make as much as she did with the print-finishing business, she loves what she does. Each bead is a tiny work of art.

Case Study

www.celiahart.co.uk

For Celia Hart, artist and illustrator, a need to spend more time helping her family provided a surprising opportunity to discover her true creative direction and start a successful business.

For many years, Celia loved working as a freelance designer and illustrator. She had dreams of further exploring her own true style but, after years of working under the direction of others, this did not come as easily to her as you might expect. While she was already working in the right career, she wasn't feeling creatively fulfilled. Then, in 2003, she went on an inspiring holiday to Japan and came back with a suitcase full of lovely hand-made paper and a sketchbook full of beautiful drawings.

This coincided with a tricky time in her and her husband's personal life because they had some very ill relatives. They were both working hard for long hours and so something had to change. Celia reduced her work dramatically so she had time to help the family. 'The time helping relatives was difficult in some ways but also allowed me some time to find mental space to work on developing my own style.' This time also helped her to work out her creative niche with her own product ranges.

Celia decided that lino prints were the perfect medium with which to develop her Japanese work and produced a beautiful set of images. She joined a local open studios event in Cambridge as a sideline and exhibited at a local small art fair in Suffolk. Another larger gallery saw her work and approached Celia asking to exhibit her prints. Then another gallery owner saw them and contacted her, and another. Before she knew it, she was observing a snowball effect of success.

Celia's time spent working as a commercial artist had also given her a clear idea of what 'worked' and what was popular. She used the time her life-changing event had offered her to use this knowledge but also to come up with a style that she loved and found a unique concept which had great commercial appeal.

Although I have suggested the ideal time for starting a business, don't be put off if you're raring to go before all the boxes are ticked. It would be much worse to be among the many would-be start-ups that never quite make it off the starting blocks because of waiting for the right time that never comes. If you really want to pursue your dream, you'll find a way to do it whatever your stage of life!

A few years before I started my own business, I was given some good advice that I'd like to pass on to you here. My good friend Triona and I decided to take some pottery evening classes in London for fun. I was feeling frustrated at work because my job wasn't all that creative and so I felt that pottery classes might help. We befriended the very talented young lady who ran the class called Hazel Faithfull. She ran a ceramics business based in Clerkenwell, where her main offering was bespoke, hand-painted pieces. She combined this with teaching to bolster her income as she loved passing on her skill and awakening talent in others.

I chatted with Hazel about the fact that I might want to design and make jewellery and start a creative business. She told me some important home truths. While it was a huge privilege being able to do what she loved, it meant that she was constantly worrying about how she was going to pay her rent. She also advised me to stick at what I know and love best.

I took Hazel's words partly as a warning – did I really want to leave my secure, lucrative job in the computer industry behind? Did I really *have* to do this? Did I have enough drive and determination to make this huge change in my life? I had to think of a way to manage things carefully.

While working in the IT industry, I had always made jewellery in my spare time, drawing a completely new and innovative design from scratch and then creating it in precious metal at my workbench. After speaking to Hazel, I decided to take the jewellery I was making more seriously in my spare time while I was still working full-time. I wanted to test how much I wanted to do this and find out if I was talented enough to design and make jewellery professionally.

I asked my dad to teach me more advanced techniques at weekends and learned others from books and from teaching myself. I wasn't going to throw in my job until I was absolutely sure I could succeed with my jewellery-making.

I have discovered that many people feel they can only learn things on training courses, from teachers or from tutors, but my creativity helps me learn things from all sorts of other places. For example, I looked at things happening in other industries. Had it been available then, I expect I would have learned some techniques from YouTube. Later, I picked up tips from the newly formed Ganoksin jewellery group, too. I felt like a sponge – hungry to soak up everything I could about jewellery and about business skills, too. The more I learned, the harder I found it to go to work in IT and the more drawn I felt to full-time jewellery design.

Looking back, I am delighted that I worked in the IT industry for those years and also very pleased that I didn't try to work professionally in the jewellery industry before I started my own business. I am sure that my lack of experience in the jewellery trade meant that I could see things with a fresh perspective and, consequently, form a different and innovative business concept.

I now always strongly advise people to try to work in a different industry first before they start a business with their true passion. In order to 'see' an industry and any gaps in the market, it really helps to come to it from a completely different angle without preconceptions about how a company in that area works.

3

Defining Success

When my son Thomas was two years old, he used to try regularly to be very assertive about which way we should go in the car, screaming that he wanted to go in the opposite direction. I tried to explain that if we went that way, we wouldn't actually get to the planned destination, but he still just wanted to go the way that looked the most interesting.

One day, I decided to go with his instinct and obeyed him, and proceeded in the wrong direction for the swimming pool. We ended up in the countryside and got out and had a bit of a walk about. He said, 'Swimming pool!' crossly. Only then did he finally understand that we had to follow the correct route to get where he wanted to go; knowing where we were going had to define how we got there.

'What does success look like to you?' is a question that I ask all of the businesses that I mentor fairly early on. Without knowing this, it is hard to help guide them because, as Thomas discovered aged two, we all need to know where we are going in order to stand any chance of getting there. Yes, you can just 'go with the flow' and that works for some, but this is more by luck than anything else. If you don't know what you are really searching for in your business, you won't really feel successful when you achieve it.

This chapter will help you figure out how to form and balance your own vision of both financial and creative success, and also identify your values.

Identifying your vision

What is your version of success? Do you just want to find a way to make money that fits around your family commitments but without taking on any more responsibility than you have to? Would you like to remain working on your own with nobody to bother you? Do you imagine a buzzing studio with a few people working with or for you? Do you hope to see your products on sale in Harrods? Do you envisage several branches? Do you imagine being a very successful, huge international luxury brand? Be honest with yourself about what you would like your creative business to bring you, and only when you can visualise it can you begin to work out how to make it into a reality.

Exercise 3

On a single A3 piece of paper, draw a picture or make a collage of images from the internet or magazines of what your ideal business would look like. What would it look like inside and out; what kind of people would work there? Consider what kind of premises you would run and whether you'd be on your own or with others. Be completely honest with yourself about what you really want out of your business. Where would your business be and what kind of reputation would you have? What would you like it to look like? How financially lucrative would you like it to be? This is an image representation of your business vision.

Exercise 4

Looking at the above image/s, summarise what you see in one or two sentences to describe your vision in words.

In my experience, everybody has difficulty crystallising their vision into a short sentence or two. However, it is important to be able to communicate this succinctly. I need to sum up my vision to business contacts or customers frequently, and it really helps when this rolls off the tongue easily. I tweak and change my vision regularly and find that the above two exercises really help me with this process.

Balancing financial and creative success

Sometimes creative and financial success can feel rather different from each other, which can be confusing. In order to pay your bills, you need to find a degree of commercial success. However, to love what you do, you also need to seek creative fulfilment. Most creative people never feel (and never want to feel) that what they produce is 100 per cent perfect, and it is this journey that inspires them to keep creating. You often need to find an overlap between commercial and creative success. The way this balance works for you is very personal and may be different from what works for others.

Some creatives weigh up each project before they accept it, balancing the commercial and creative aspects on a case by case basis. For example, some projects might be creatively fulfilling and great for your profile, even though they don't bring you much income. Others may be creatively bland but lucrative. I have always worked like this, especially early on in my business journey. There were projects that I took which I knew would only just pay for their own materials but would be talked about, get press and give me a good 'story' for my website. Even now, I occasionally take on projects which are not going to earn enough but which feel right for us to work on for other reasons, such as designing and making a ring to promote Fairtrade gold that we knew we would not sell as it displayed their logo.

As you can see in the following case study, Keith Brymer Jones tries to find projects that bring him enough of each type of success:

Case Study

Keith Brymer Jones, the ceramicist, advises that you should weigh up projects, seeking those that are both creatively exciting and work commercially. He also finds that his newer definition of success includes giving opportunities to new designers.

In many ways, Keith does not yet feel all that successful despite having a thriving business and being a known name on national television. 'When you're creative, even when you have done well, you always only feel 98 per cent good about it but never 100 per cent; nothing is ever perfect! As long as you realise that, you can always try to attain perfection and perhaps really this is why we creatives keep creating and trying to strive for the summit.'

Keith feels that to reach success, you need to be able to pay your bills and live comfortably and, beyond that, you need to be happy in what you do. His work doesn't feel like a job to him because he loves it so much.

Keith also advises that as a business person, you have to weigh up every project that comes along, seeking projects which are both exciting and will work commercially while also weighing up what fits with your ethics, creativity and credibility. However, as your business thrives and your success grows, the risks can seem to keep growing and it can become harder to feel successful as your vision of how success is defined also changes. He says, 'When I think about success in terms of what makes me feel happy, at the moment I'd say that what I love the most is finding designers and giving them opportunities that they couldn't create on their own. These young designers also inspire me. I love the idea that we could give a designer a start that might turn out to be the next Cath Kidston or something; it just feels great to be helping them start their creative journey.'

If the balance between creative and financial success tips too far towards commercial success and away from creative fulfilment, it can feel very frustrating. Nobody wants to be churning out work that feels unfulfilling or boring. This is particularly true for those of us who create things with our hands because we put so much of ourselves into our work, so it can feel soul destroying to be making pieces which do not feel exciting or challenging, just to pay the bills. However every creative I have spoken to has, at some point, put up with some less exciting works to make some money and to enable them to work on more appealing projects afterwards.

Laura Sparling, the designer of lampwork beads, explains how she juggles creatively fulfilling and commercially successful products. She strives to achieve both in one project and, when she can make this work, this defines success for her.

Laura's definition of success involves making the things that she really wants to create and finding people who want to buy those pieces. She feels success is defined by managing not to bend herself too much towards what customers want her to make and staying true to what she wants to make.

She finds that there are some steady sellers in her product range like strings of plain beads and polka dot beads. She doesn't enjoy making them and finds this work rather boring but often needs to spend a few days working on these as they sell well. However, over time, this can end up making her work feel too much like a chore and she finds she can get stuck in a rut. She likes to remind people that everybody has bad days at work including creative entrepreneurs, saying, 'I do love it, but running a business isn't all laughs and giggles – there are also days when I want to throw the laptop out the window.' But then she remembers that she still really loves lampworking and much prefers her lifestyle to working in a shop or an office.

So Laura counters this by making what she really wants to make as often as possible so that she doesn't risk losing her passion. She really enjoys making the more elaborately decorated beads and finds this kind of work really rewarding. As you will read in the chapter on marketing, she finds innovative ways to highlight these more to her market so that she can make more of them. So she strikes a balance between making what the market wants and making what she loves to keep her passion alive. She says, 'It is brilliant when I put something

I've enjoyed creating on my website and then they sell out really fast; then I get a taste of real fulfilment.' As her business develops and her talent as a bead artist becomes more recognised, she is able to do this more and more.

Many creatives aspire to doing large, exciting or ambitious projects but these don't come along very often, especially when you are starting up. So sometimes finding the balance between financial and creative success needs some introspective soul searching to come up with a different way of looking at or enjoying smaller projects.

As I have told my design team in the past, while we would love to be making huge, high-budget, ready-to-wear necklaces, there simply isn't a market for these at the moment and, of course, we can't just make these simply to take apart all of that hard and expensive work a year later when they haven't sold. I used to think that this was just to do with the fact that we weren't big enough or well known enough to do this kind of work, but I recently chatted to three separate, extremely high-end, famous jewellers who told me that they almost never sell their large, ready-to-wear, expensive necklaces either! They just make them for advertising campaigns and as something for their customers to aspire to but possibly never acquire. So instead of feeling frustrated about not being able to make and sell something huge, it may be better to reconsider what stretches you as an artist and see if you can find a new way of feeling fulfilled and successful within the commercial projects that are coming to you. Can you use your creativity differently but in an equally fulfilling way?

Many years ago, I remember the moment when I realised that it was much harder to design and make the perfect *low-budget* bespoke engagement ring than to work with larger funds. So I consciously decided to see this low-budget challenge as an exciting creative problem to solve. Once I switched into this new way of thinking, I loved it and the customer loved what I came up with. After that, our brand really took off.

Steve Shipman, wedding photographer, finds that he defines success as the satisfaction that he gets from producing work that he is happy with and which also pleases his clients. He finds ways to achieve this success even within less obviously inspiring shoots.

Steve has got his business to a point where he feels it is successful and it sustains his lifestyle and business position. But what about creative success – how does Steve define that?

'For me, it is the satisfaction that you get from producing work that you are happy in creating but which also pleases your clients. When those two things come together, then that is the dream in a creative business. I do also shoot a lot of personal work which is also satisfying. But when you have to shoot a wedding which might not be the most spectacular one but you manage to find angles and a way to get really great creative shots and the client is delighted, this is so rewarding. It is all about finding the gems.'

Steve also gets a lot of creative and business satisfaction from teaching and sharing. 'I love seeing new photographers coming through and trying to help people get on to the right path for their business.'

Ethical vision

There are many businesses which thrive while pursuing less conventional models of success. For example, perhaps social, ethical or environmental concerns are a large part of their vision and inspire their creativity.

These issues have always been a significant driver for me and my business and I could never have relaxed into creative fulfilment while I knew that the materials that I was working with may have been mined at gunpoint or relied upon forced child labour.

If your ideas fit into this category, you might also want to consider setting your own business up as a social enterprise rather than a conventional business like Rosie Ginday's:

Miss Macaroon 🍲

Success for Rosie Ginday from Miss Macaroon, who make hand-crafted macaroons, comes in the form of a social enterprise but she also keeps an eye on traditional business measures and both culinary and business creativity.

While Rosie creates beautiful and delicious macaroons, she also has a social purpose in mind. She feels that her creative business is very successful on all fronts. 'It is a social enterprise, so I'm really driven by providing training and jobs for young people who have been long-term unemployed, which is very important to how we define success. But we are also cash positive and profitable and, in six years, we have grown to three sites: the training site, the production kitchen and now a retail space and Prosecco bar. We've recently doubled the size of our team to ten. So all of the traditional measures of business success are looking good, too. This retail space is already developing the wonderful community atmosphere that I always envisioned. The business is always growing and changing so I am constantly learning and having to be creative, which I love.'

In contrast to Rosie, when I talk to many creative business people who align themselves with an ethical or social vision, they often say that they do not feel very financially successful, even though they love what they do. Some tell me that although they are getting by and paying the bills, they could easily double what they earn by getting a 'proper job' elsewhere and this confuses them as they feel frustrated when they compare their income to that of their friends. I advise these people not to think like this as they can end up in a downward spiral. Instead, they need to remember that their definition of success is not only financial and that their gratification is made from different elements. There are so many other things that running a creative and ethical business can bring them. Their well-off friends don't usually get to choose their hours and location, do what they love for a living, seek creative fulfilment and change the world.

Celia Persephone Gregory, artist, sculptor and marine conservationist, finds that aligning with a creative definition of success rather than just a financial one feels more rewarding.

Celia's vision for The Marine Foundation is to support, value, respect and appreciate the resources and pleasures that the oceans provide through fun and creativity. She achieves this because her stunning underwater sculptures are widely shared on social networks and are made from a special material that supports marine life.

When I asked her about success, Celia said, 'In terms of lifestyle and what I have achieved creatively and environmentally, yes, I do feel very successful. When I think in financial terms, this aspect of my business does not feel so successful. When you run a creative business you can have the lifestyle that you want and you can create things, and aligning with a definition of success like this can really work. Aligning with a definition of success that is entirely financial might mean that you deny yourself fulfilment.'

Celia feels that creating things for a living defines who she is. 'I can't not do it because it is inherently part of me.' She thinks of her ability to market her work as an entirely separate thing that defines her financial rewards.

Defining your business values

An important tool that I began to use a number of years ago was to carefully define our business values. In this way, I set out part of our definition of success for everybody to see. First, I took a long, hard look at my own personal vision for the business and articulated this into eight principles. They took quite a while to write down clearly and carefully, but have been instrumental in my business to the extent that I now suggest to every start-up to do this early on.

We hold everything that we do up against this set of values to check that it fits before going ahead. Now they are on my website for all to see. We recruit by them, too, so that we can be sure that all of our team members want to drive in the same direction as the rest of us.

Exercise 5

Browse online for lists of business values or business philosophies for brands or restaurants that you admire (you will find that they are often set out on company websites). Use these as research and have a go at writing five or more values of your own. Remember that to work well they need to come from your heart.

Here are some examples of values that other creatives have defined:

- I believe in traditional techniques but like to communicate them using cutting-edge technology

- I strive to make each product give its owner joy and visual balance

- I want every client to enjoy the experience of buying my creations almost as much as they value the creations themselves

- I believe in quality and strive to be the best and for my products only to be available through channels of similar quality

- I will source the most environmentally and socially responsible materials that I can find

Having confidence in your vision

Your vision will be highly personal to you. It is important not to let others influence you too much with this. You might be quite happy with a small premises with one or two people helping you and, if so, don't get swept away because your partner wants you to have several shops and a TV series. Conversely, don't let the limitations and expectations of others hold you back. The truth is that you can achieve anything you want if you stay clear about what you are striving for.

When your vision and values are clear, they can join together to help you forge a completely new pathway in business. When you are starting the journey, it can be confusing and hard to spot obstacles in the path towards your definition of success. Many creatives find that they want to blaze a completely new trail but lack the confidence in their idea to believe this is really possible. Sometimes, gaining confidence in yourself and in your vision is an important and time-consuming early part of your business and creative journey.

I spent the first months of my jewellery business thinking that if I was to run a jewellery business it had to be rather like a different copy of another jewellery business. It took a 'wake-up call' for me to believe whole-heartedly that even though there weren't any jewellers making reachable – i.e. affordable and easily accessible – bespoke jewellery at the time, there really was a market ready to receive my business offering in this arena. Even though I had a waiting list of thirty-three customers wanting bespoke projects, I still didn't quite believe the customer demand that was staring me in the face! I had to believe in my own vision and trailblaze for a whole new section in my industry. It is hard to have that kind of confidence in your vision when you are just one creative person working alone on an untrodden pathway.

Creative people often see new connections and pioneer whole new offerings that have not previously existed. You need to be clear and confident in your vision of success before you can have the kind of confidence to achieve such a thing. Copying a conventional business model does not always work for people with creative minds and this is not usually a way to find and carve out a new creative business niche, as Mohammed Jamal found:

22ct GOLD GUILT 19g TOP

OLIVE CUT

HAND BLOW CRYSTAL BOTTLE.

Mohammed Jamal, of Jamal Perfumers London, explains how he couldn't feel successful and build his business confidence until he really examined his values and realised that he was blocking his own vision by trying to fit it into a conventional business model.

After spending years becoming highly qualified, creating four artisan scents and building his start-up, Mohammed felt that his branding was not communicating his craftsmanship nor his perfumery heritage well, and his scents didn't feel successful to him. In rethinking his brand communication strategy, he began to re-evaluate his entire business model and realised that he had lost sight of his own vision, values and definition of success.

When starting up, Mohammed kept being told that to bring a product to market you have to have a lot of money, find the right people and do the right PR and marketing. However, he couldn't quite reconcile this with what he was achieving, because he hadn't fully aligned his own vision and purpose yet. He explains, 'Finding my aptitude and my most inner zone of happiness and contentment has been key to really understanding my own vision and defining what I need to feel truly successful.'

When Mohammed looks back, he feels that he was blocking his own pathway by mistakenly believing that, regardless of his vision, he had to have a product in a department store to be successful.

Mohammed urges creative founders not to let a conventional administrative fingerprint dictate how your business should be or how your creativity should be delivered. He says, 'I found out that is the wrong way to form a creative business. Once I had kicked that out of my way, the burden was gone and then I soon found that I was genuinely excited and walking along the right path towards my real vision of success.'

Now that he is truly following his vision, Mohammed wakes up every day with a purpose. He enjoys what he does and his values help him give back to people along his supply chain and help improve their lives through perfumery, which has also further enriched his brand. He says, 'My vision includes how I add value to greater humanity and this gives me satisfaction by seeing others doing well, as everybody wants to feel that special self-worth.'

Once you have decided on your vision and your values, you can confidently hold everything that you do up to them and check that it fits. In order to be true to your values and vision, you have to be very strong and sometimes even say 'no' to opportunities. This is very hard to do and I can't say that I was very good at it in my early days as it takes significant courage.

The next case study is an interesting example of the kind of certainty it sometimes takes to be true to your vision.

Case Study

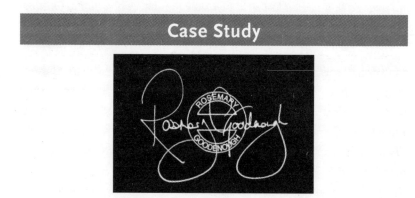

Rosemary Goodenough, an artist whose work encompasses art, fashion and lifestyle, had a clear vision to build a recognised heritage luxury brand while remaining true to her art. This unerring clarity means that she is unafraid to say 'no' where necessary to realise her definition of success.

Rosemary is an artist who moves between genres, adapting to different media depending on the project and what feels right. Michael

Waller-Bridge, Rosemary's husband, is a professional photographer and he takes great images of Rosemary's artwork which she then digitally colours and adapts while remaining true to the original composition. These images are printed on to silk in Italy to create their products. 'It all comes from my art; all scarves have to come from paintings but not all paintings will become scarves. I'm not a scarf designer who paints in order to create a product; I don't paint for the scarves.' The value of only creating products from her fine art is core to Rosemary's definition of success.

Rosemary had to take a significant leap when investing in product ranges. 'It was a risk, particularly at my age as Michael and I are both in our early sixties. The minimum order in these high-quality silks was frightening. However, not doing it felt like more of a risk because I could so clearly envision the extraordinary possibilities. I realised that my vision could not only be about creating beautiful things but also creating a successful brand.'

I was fascinated to discover how carefully Rosemary designs every brand detail. For example, she spent days deciding on exactly what the tissue paper used to wrap the products would sound like, not stopping until she felt she'd achieved her vision of the perfect packaging.

Rosemary thinks carefully about how and where she wants her work to appear. 'Saying "no" is not always a negative thing and walking away is sometimes a very positive thing to do in order to keep brand vision and channels exactly right.' Over the last four years, she has declined numerous offers to be stocked in certain stores where the environment did not seem right or if the potential collaborators didn't share her eye for detail. Similarly, she doesn't want to see her artwork on cheaper products like plastic make-up bags, saying, 'We have to be very careful not to compromise. We give ideas the "elegance and sophistication" test – if they pass this test and feel true to our brand, then they are good.'

It isn't always easy to walk away from these kinds of opportunities and I don't think that I was as strong in my early business years as Rosemary. However, her unerring confidence in her vision and in her brand has helped Rosemary steer her course towards her own success.

Growing and changing your vision

As many of the case studies in this chapter have illustrated, it is possible for your vision to change over time, just as mine did. When I started out, I dreamed of having a small studio where I worked with four or five others. When I achieved that, I found that my vision had grown, too. Over the last twenty years, it has probably morphed and changed about four times so far, perhaps because achieving my vision makes me aware of further possibilities; not for me personally, but for my entire committed and brilliant team. However, you still need to know what you are aiming for at any one time.

4

Creating Your Product Idea

It is extremely rare for somebody to be so creatively gifted that their products can stand out in a crowded market because of just their talent and style. This applies to only very few: the awesomely talented, the exceptionally lucky and the very well connected. When you want to start a business to sell your work, you really need to have a good product idea for which there is also a real 'gap in the market' for what you offer. In this chapter, we will examine what this means and look at different ways in which many creatives find their 'gap'.

Finding the gap

When planning a product range, it is best to assume that your own unique style is not enough to forge a gap in the market. Most of us need an idea that somehow contains our creativity in a 'difference' to be financially successful; i.e. we need something that makes our products stand out and makes them special to our customers. Simply making things in your own particular style may work for you as an artist, but is rarely enough for you to be able actually to make a living, at least at first. I've lost count of the number of failed creative businesses who tried to sell their versions of products that were not different enough from others.

Interestingly, once you have trailblazed your path and have found a degree of success, you can gradually move your business over to be even more fulfilling to your creative needs. But at least at first, I would advise walking a careful path between your market and your creativity. You need to keep an eye on what the market wants and you also need to have a level of creative fulfilment. Focusing on either one of those two things too much is unlikely to work.

So harness your creativity to find a real gap, both in what you do, and how you approach the market. You may not need an innovative gap in both of these, but it helps. In my opinion, you need at least one. I believe that most of us need a clear 'new' path or story in some way in order to make sure you can actually pay your rent.

So what kind of idea might be different enough to be defined as forging a niche in the market? What is it that will make your creative expression into a product or offering that makes it stand out and is hard for other businesses to copy? Here are a few different ways in which creative businesses can find their niche.

Innovation through combining previously separate concepts

New products regularly emerge when previously known concepts are used in innovative ways or combined to give birth to something ground-breaking. Who could have predicted that coloured elastic bands could get kids everywhere weaving loom band jewellery a few years ago, or that sequins could be formatted to be directionally brushed? But five-minute wonders aside, there is a lot to be learned by looking at what you do and combining it with something unexpected or perhaps allowing your audience to help you evolve an innovative product.

The artist Rosemary Goodenough combined her art work with textiles to find her first innovative product range.

Rosemary already has a very successful career as an artist, but when she overheard a lady at an exhibition commenting that she'd like to wear one of Rosemary's paintings as a scarf, she began to envisage a completely different business direction.

With her high-quality, fine silk twill scarves, Rosemary had some success at trade shows and was picked up by some leading stores like Fortnum & Mason. However, she found that the market for ladies' scarves was extremely crowded with every luxury brand selling a line of neckwear, so it was hard to find some space in this sector.

Over the next eighteen months, she found that more of her high-quality scarves were being worn by men than women, which showed her a new way forward. She then came up with a completely new concept for the neck-tie and was recently told by Paul Alger, International Director of the UK Fashion and Textile Association, that she is the first person to redesign the neck-tie in over 150 years.

It takes a special kind of creativity and drive to merge previously uncombined concepts. It can take enormous bravery to do this on a really large and dramatic scale. The next case study is an example of just that and I also think that it can teach valuable lessons on taking risks, pricing and spotting a great patron. It also shows that occasionally you can find a gap in the market in a rather unconventional way if you follow a project you really believe in and it is viewed by the right people.

Dominic and Frances Bromley from Scabetti combined their ceramics with lighting and installation to find their product idea, which also showed them a gap in the market. However, to fulfil their vision, they had to combine these elements on a huge scale which meant risking everything.

Dominic and Frances had been promoting various earthenware and bone china pieces. When exhibiting at a trade show in 2004, they wanted to make their exhibition space stand out, so they developed 'Drawn to the Light', a suspended sculpture with a light at its centre. This idea of using light and suspended ceramics was refreshing at the time and drew a lot of attention and press, so they realised that this concept had significant potential beyond just pulling crowds to their stand. They developed it into a collection of products and, by 2007, 'Shoal' was born, featuring a column of 284 fish.

Feeling the excitement that Shoal created, they saw it had even more potential and decided to enter it into the 100% Design trade show competition, where the winners would receive a large space to exhibit their design free of charge at the brand-new section of the show called '100% Futures'.

After many long days and late nights working on the pitch, they were thrilled when their proposal for a 2m tall and 1.5m diameter Shoal with 1,672 fish won the competition. However, they still had to put in more energy and investment to make and install this ambitious piece. They decided to risk everything, taking a loan out against their house. They even talked of packing in the creative business and opening a greengrocer's shop if they couldn't pull it off.

They were still making the piece the day before the exhibition opened and only worked out their pricing on the morning of the show. Frances calculated the price and Dominic worried that if they had to charge such a high price, it would never sell. Frances pointed out, however, that they couldn't afford to sell it for any less because that would mean they'd be making a loss, so they nervously pressed on.

Shoal was a huge hit at the show, much to their relief. Alongside the sale of their original sculpture, they received two other significant orders. One was from Jill and Rick Stein for their world-famous Seafood Restaurant in Cornwall, and another was by a prominent architect working on the International Maritime Organisation's headquarters in London. Without doubt, these orders helped to put Scabetti's Shoal series of products and installations on the design map.

When Jill Stein spotted the sculpture at the trade show, she loved it, but their restaurant was due to open in just a few months so quick thinking was needed, as they hadn't budgeted for such an installation. Dominic and Frances trusted their instincts, sensing Jill's belief in their work. They bravely offered the sculpture on loan, saying that if the Steins weren't totally happy after a year, they would take it away again. This was a clever risk; good design of this scale has to be seen to be appreciated and this was the perfect platform for Shoal to be seen by a completely new coastal market. Frances and Dominic foresaw that this could result in more much needed sales. The Steins were delighted with Shoal and the welcome it gave their guests and paid for it in full within just a few months. Frances adds, 'There are some lovely people out there, like Rick and Jill, who are honest and honourable and really do just want you to succeed.'

Frances and Dominic soon discovered that the number of influential and high-profile people who choose to dine at Jill and Rick Stein's restaurant is extraordinary. This, along with their launch of Shoal at an International Design Exhibition, raised their profile hugely.

After this roller-coaster ride, Frances advises creative entrepreneurs, 'If you feel you come out winning . . . then you have won, even if others think you haven't got the best deal. When you put your heart and soul into your creative ideas, every time somebody buys from you, it's like a pat on the back and this recognition can be very important.'

Frances speculates that had she been researching the coastal market, then Shoal would have been the perfect answer to this brief. However, this isn't actually how it happened. Instead, they took a huge risk and put *something 'out there' that they really believed in. They discovered there was a big market for their innovative piece that they had not previously identified. Their path to success was highly unconventional but they found a real gap in the market via a scenic and slightly scary route.*

New technology

Embracing new technology can be creatively interesting and, if you are an early adopter, this can also mean you are ahead of a wave. The trick here is to trust your instincts on which new technology is likely to stick and to use it to inspire your creativity to flourish in a new way.

The next two case studies are examples of how two creatives adopted digital technology early in completely different ways, which I think should inspire us all to think inventively.

Case Study

The wedding photographer Steve Shipman found his business idea in a new approach to wedding photography.

Steve was first an editorial photographer working in glossy magazines doing centre spreads or cover shots for magazines like the Sunday Times Magazine *and* Cosmopolitan. *Then he started doing a lot of corporate work which was less creative, so he needed to change direction.*

In 2001, the digital photography revolution was having a huge influence, triggering a move away from posed photography. No longer did you have to be constrained by the cost of film and processing each shot. Even though the first professional cameras were expensive – Steve's cost him £8,000 – and you couldn't fit much on a memory card, it enabled photographers to shoot loads of images with great freedom to experiment. This led Steve to a completely new style of photography which was more casual, less posed and involved capturing interesting moments.

When Steve was asked to help a friend to shoot a wedding, they were amazed to discover that they absolutely loved it. He found that he could record a wedding day in a completely new, fun and lively way, being both discreet and creative.

So for Steve, the introduction of digital photography and the timing of starting his business all came together perfectly. This led to him discovering that he loves capturing emotions, which fits perfectly with the wedding market. So his 'big idea' was bringing this to the market with new technology at the right time.

Case Study

Richard Weston of Weston Earth Images combined cutting-edge, digital, close-up photography with textiles to find a highly successful product direction.

Richard was a professor of architecture at Cardiff University but he had another passion for the 'designs' found in nature. At first, he used the latest digital technology to take very close-up images of natural materials (especially semi-precious gemstones) as a hobby. He partnered up with Martin Price and they began trying to sell the images as wall artwork.

Richard had a gut feeling that the images would work particularly well on fabrics and wanted to get them printed on to silk. However, his first attempts to break into the fashion industry failed, with buyers saying that because his patterns were natural and didn't have a regular repeat, they would never work as fabrics. However, his passion for driving his big idea forward was relentless, because he felt strongly that these beautiful natural images had to be shared.

Then he hit the headlines in 2011 following a TV appearance on BBC2 in Britain's Next Big Thing, with silk scarves printed with his designs. His first scarves sold at Liberty, among other high-end retailers. Suddenly, everybody had heard of him and there was a demand for his work.

I own one of Richard's scarves and, aside from my jewellery, it is my most frequently admired piece of clothing. When I tell people that it is a close-up of a gemstone called fluorite, their eyes widen because the story makes it all the more interesting. The fact that these are extreme close-ups of natural forms is very special and the combination of these factors gave him his 'big idea'.

Becoming a specialist

Sometimes your business niche can be born not from doing more, but by offering less diversity in the form of specialisation. It can feel like a very brave decision to stop offering some of your work, but it is often a wise move. When Children's Supermart, a baby furniture retailer, dropped furniture, specialised in toys and rebranded as Toys "R" Us, they really began to find success and became a household name for more than sixty years.

Perhaps your specialism could be working in very specific materials or in ethical sourcing. Perhaps you can offer bespoke pieces or target a very specific market need which is not yet being addressed.

Could focusing on specific elements of your work be your key to your business or product idea?

Case Study

Nanna Sandom of Splendid Stitches found that specialising in vintage alterations and dropping other work improved her business, resulting in her big idea.

Nanna originally started her business offering all kinds of clothing alterations, wanting to focus on keeping clothes out of landfill. This was a broad idea and, in an era before sustainable fashion, it was hard for her to achieve focused marketing. There are a lot of all-round alteration services competing in a low-price-point market and offering poor-quality work, from which Nanna wanted to disconnect herself.

Her real passion is for vintage clothing, which is obvious when you speak with her about her projects and look at her own clothing. But it took some good business advice to help her realise that she should just focus on this specific aspect of the alterations market. This was perfect for Nanna; not only was this a gap in the market, but she also really enjoys creatively bringing out the true strengths of any vintage piece. This speciality or niche allows her to really focus her business activities.

Case Study

Rosie Ginday of Miss Macaroon offers highly specialised products with bespoke and last-minute options, as well as incorporating a specialist social enterprise ethic at the core of the business. It is interesting to discover how she formed and gradually crystallised her business ideas to marry up these different elements.

While studying at sixth form, Rosie waitressed and got talking to local homeless people, including one young man who had lost everything in a house fire and then his mum died, leaving him on the streets. Rosie decided that she wanted to do something to help people like him. After studying art at university, travelling and starting a community restaurant in Taiwan, she envisioned teaching young unemployed people kitchen skills.

Rosie quickly qualified and got some experience in a Michelin-starred restaurant, spending her free time hatching her business idea and creating and developing recipes. She fell in love with macaroons, which were complicated enough to be challenging but with fillings made with a fairly simple recipe, so that people new to cooking could learn through making them. She also found that they allow a lot of creativity with infinite flavour and colour combinations. Having watched a recent trend take off for cupcakes in fashionable cities, she felt that she might be able to start the next patisserie trend and specialise in macaroons, with the business also specifically helping young unemployed people build their confidence. Miss Macaroon was born in 2011 when Rosie was 26 years old.

Rosie knew that just having great patisserie was not going to be enough to appeal to the market and grow her creative and social vision. She needed further differences to make her business truly flourish, and gradually came up with several other ways to make Miss Macaroon's offerings stand out even more through enhanced specialisation. Drawing on her art background and knowledge of colour theory, she developed a method to colour match the macaroons to any Pantone shade. She also focused on being able to provide bespoke packaging, bespoke logos on the macaroons and fulfilling last-minute orders.

If you choose to specialise as a business like Rosie or Nanna, you really need to think fully about your expert subject so that you offer far more than any other business who might cover your area as a smaller part of what they do. For example, my business specialises in bespoke jewellery, but other jewellers now sometimes offer this as just part of what they do, too. However, because we are experts in this area, all of our processes and team members are highly focused towards bespoke. So, for example, each customer works with their own dedicated, degree-qualified designer. We will provide photograph books of our goldsmiths making each bespoke piece, we are experts in re-using our customers' own materials creatively and we will fully educate our customers on the different gemstones they choose. And we are constantly trying to think of new ways to further enhance our bespoke speciality.

So specialising enables you to focus your business activities, but also means that you need to form a higher level of expertise in that particular area of your craft, giving people a compelling reason to choose you as *the* specialist. And that is exactly what I did with my own bespoke jewellery business. I found that my own 'big idea' was designing and making reachable bespoke jewellery but it took me a while to realise that this was the right direction for me.

Michael, my boss in the IT industry, admired the jewellery that I made and wore and this led to him giving me one of my very first commissions; I was to design a modern, unusual brooch for his wife to celebrate their wedding anniversary. He originally asked me to just make him a nice brooch, but I suggested specially designing something for him inspired by fireworks because they had originally met on 5 November. I drew a page of design options and he chose his favourite which I made for him.

I really liked collaborating with a client in this way, and working with my first few customers like this showed me that this was a really stimulating and different way of working. Why should customers have to choose from a range when they could each have something individually made for them?

My market research was built from 'trying it out' while still working in my full-time day job. Looking back, this was probably the best kind of market research I could have done. What I was offering was very different; I would provide an individual design service and then make the pieces within budget, too. Crucially, this was not being offered anywhere else.

I had seen a gap in the market for reachable bespoke jewellery which was designed and made specially for each customer. Back then, this was not something that ordinary people could afford – yes, you might know a goldsmith with a jewellery bench who could make what you'd asked, but they would not design something that perfectly suited your style and brief and then make you something that not only fitted your budget but also left you tearful with joy.

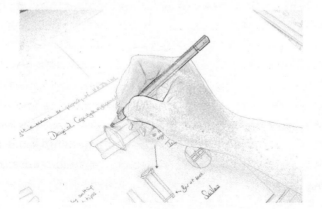

I also found a new route to market via the Internet, which is something I'll cover in more detail in later chapters. Very few jewellers anywhere were offering any kind of commission service at all, and I certainly wasn't aware of any other jewellers of any kind on the Internet back then.

I looked at different words to use. My grandmother had been a 'bespoke tailor', so I landed on the word 'bespoke' but I was worried about it because it wasn't widely understood and also isn't an international word. I was also concerned that it might sound a bit pretentious. However, I felt it was the best word I could come up with and so decided to use it. So we put the previously unused phrase 'Bespoke Jewellery' on the website and it stuck.

At first, we had to explain the word 'bespoke' on our website, too, because nobody knew what it meant. Customers were used to only being able to choose pieces from the shelf in jewellery shops and they could hardly believe it when I explained that I would actually make something specially for them and from scratch. So underneath that phrase I'd write something like 'Making jewellery especially for you to suit your style, personality and budget'. The word 'bespoke' has caught on extensively in the jewellery industry and is used a lot in the wider world, too, now.

It is probably a longer story for another book, but we endeavoured to find more ethical suppliers aligned with our core values, and so we became the first company in the world to be both certified by the Responsible Jewellery Council and licensed to use Fairtrade gold. This has also given us a point of difference from other jewellers, which was a surprise and not something that I realised would eventually differentiate us. At first we were just 'doing the right thing' quietly, but we discovered that clients were really interested in this, too.

Creating a difference

As you can see from these stories, market gaps come in all shapes and sizes. You might have found a niche like Dominic and Frances or Richard Weston, combining techniques or concepts creatively and using them in a completely innovative way. You might have found a niche like me, in personalisation that had never previously been available. Are you driving forward with a great social or ethical difference like Rosie

Ginday? Or, like Steve, maybe you will harness new technology in a way that really works for your emotional connection with your work. This is what I mean when I advise you to harness your creativity, not only in what you can do, but also how you connect with your market. Think about how you can forge yourself the right path. Only then does a creative passion become a 'big idea'.

There are other facets that you can add to your creativity to help your 'big idea' emerge, too. For example, it may be that you are able to produce your work more quickly than others. Or perhaps you can make something in a more ethical or environmentally friendly way and you intend this to be part of what makes your offering special. Or perhaps you plan customer service that will be unbeatable and you want to combine that with other ideas of yours to forge your niche.

Some businesses succeed by focusing on a price difference and manage to produce something much more cheaply than others. However, a price-based business model is particularly hard to follow in creative industries and you are often wiser to stick with a higher-end approach to your market.

Once you think you know what your 'big idea' will be, it is important to think about how you can easily put it into words. In my experience, the best business ideas can be neatly summed up in a sentence. Sorry about the slightly nauseating term, but many like to call this their 'elevator pitch' – i.e. if you are standing in a lift with somebody, can you explain your business idea to them in a sentence or two between floors?

Exercise 6

In your personal notebook, provide the answers to the following questions. Some examples have been provided below.

- What do I do?

- How is it different?

- What is good about it?

- Why can't it easily be copied?

Example

What do I do? Make beautiful handbags.

How is it different? They have several different fascia design options for each bag that you can change. Also the fabrics are made by an African social women's group.

What is good about it? You can easily change your bag over to match your outfit without having to move everything round. They are also very colourful and unusual. The ethical credentials of my bags are also very important to me.

Why can't it easily be copied? The fabrics are distinctive; the bag-making process is quite labour intensive and so can't easily be mass-produced.

Exercise 7

From the above exercise, narrow down the key elements to develop your elevator pitch. It must be no more than two sentences long and must sum up what you do and why it is special.

Example

I create beautiful handbags from colourful fabrics made by an African women's co-operative, which are interchangeable so that you can quickly transform your bag to match your outfit as often as you like.

Now that you have your elevator pitch, test it with friends and people you meet. Does it feel right? You may need to adapt it a little while you perfect it, but remember to write it down when you are completely happy.

You will also use this pitch every day to communicate quickly what you do to everybody you know. In this way, you can begin to use your own personal network to spread the word about your start-up.

As your business grows and develops, you will need this more and more, whether it be to chat to potential suppliers, to sell to customers or to insert in a job advert when you need some help. You should include it in your business plan, social media profiles and on your website.

5

Identifying Your Market

So you think you have your product and business idea and your friends have probably told you it is a sure bet, too. You are excited to get on with it – right? But slow down; stop and check first.

In this chapter, you will learn about the value of good-quality market research to check if you are investing your time, energy and money in something that will actually sell. You can get so carried away with your idea that you can easily forge ahead with the wrong concept and waste time and money trying to find a market that does not really exist.

Designing for your market

When you are thinking about going into business, you need to offer what your customers want, not just do what you fancy and hope that customers will like it. This is the thing I most frequently hear myself telling the creatives that I have mentored over the years. It is extremely rare for anybody to be able to create a market around their offering; success is much more likely when feeding a hungry market with what it already wants.

So the key here is to think about your customer first and then create your business offering around what they want, not the other way round. So thinking about your potential customers is actually part of the 'big idea', and you need to cycle between this chapter and the last one until everything fits.

If you are truly creative, you should be able to find a way to enjoy the creativity within the demands of the market; it is not about trying to encourage customers to desire what you want to make. And when I started my bespoke jewellery business, I realised quite early on that solid market research, and keeping an open mind, are vital, and can help you avoid making costly errors. I thought I had my big idea, but I was wrong. I then did some 'market research' to try to convince myself that it was the right idea. So here is how *not* to interpret market research.

Now it seems completely obvious that I should have just carried on doing what was already working for me by designing and making commissions for people. However, there was no other model that I could use as a template in which somebody was designing and making bespoke jewellery for the general public as an entire business. So I remember thinking that if nobody was already running a small business based on designing and making commissioned jewellery, then there must have been a reason that this kind of enterprise could not work. So I didn't consider that path properly at first, overlooking the fact that this was a business idea in itself. I thought that starting a business full-time meant that I needed to do something along similar lines to other established jewellery manufacturers.

I knew I had to find a gap in the market and I realised that customisation might be that niche. I spent hours looking around high-street jewellers and jewellery galleries and came up with the idea that my business should specialise in making made-to-measure gold and silver chains with the option of semi-precious beads being set into the chain work. There wasn't anything like this available elsewhere, so I imagined providing this customisable service either directly to customers or through other retailers, like department stores.

I summoned up all of my courage and took a clipboard out to the high street of a local town to do some research to see if there was a market for this. I laugh now when I think about it as this whole research project was utterly flawed! I was so convinced that my idea was a good one that I was blinded to any other reality. I was going to make my research prove my idea was valid by hook or by crook!

That long day on the high street, I must have spoken to about three hundred people and I had asked them all my ten leading questions about whether they might like the idea of customisable, chain-based jewellery. Despite the fact that most of these people had said they really wouldn't buy this, I only heard the few who said that they liked the idea. Looking back, they were probably only saying this to humour me anyway. However, when I came up with a leaflet advertising this service and dropped it through hundreds of doors, I only sold one piece of jewellery to a family friend. It was a disaster. My market research was completely flawed.

Market research

With hindsight, my story was a really good lesson in how *not* to do market research. I asked leading questions which would never have revealed that there wasn't a market for my made-to-measure chains with semi-precious beads. I only had tentative suggestions that people liked the products I showed them, and didn't give them a chance to say they wouldn't buy them; I made it far too easy for them to say they liked them in order to be polite and far too difficult to say they wouldn't buy them. Then I chose not to listen to those brave enough to suggest that, while they liked them, they probably wouldn't buy them.

So here is how *not* to do market research:

- Don't ask leading questions

- Make sure it is easy for people to give honest opinions without feeling rude

- Really listen to what your potential customers say

- Don't just hear what you want to hear

You can't just make a gap in the market where one doesn't exist, however hard you try to convince yourself otherwise! Your ideas and products are unlikely to change anyone's mind. Had I realised this, I would not have wasted the few months that followed.

Jewellery commissions kept coming to me via word of mouth, but I was still convinced that this part of my business was just a sideline. I was still convinced that the customisable chain idea was going to be the main core of my business. It wasn't until I received some very good business advice a couple of months later that the penny dropped.

When you are starting out with a business idea, it is easy to fall into this trap. I wanted to believe my first business idea was viable, so much so that I inadvertently biased the outcome of my market research.

You definitely *should* do market research to test your idea, but learn from my mistake and do it properly.

Visualising your customers

One good way to start thinking about your market is to visualise who might like to buy your pieces or your products. What do they look like? What kind of house do they live in? What do they do in the evenings and at weekends and what kind of employment do they have? Who are their friends? What binds them together?

The customers of some companies fall into a particular geographical area or into a particular income bracket and age range. Our customers at the jewellery studio are a bit different in that they don't seem to fall into a particular income bracket or lifestyle. They share an 'attitude' rather than an age range. However, that attitude is still something that we can describe and it is what brings them together as a group of people. For example, we find that they almost always have some kind of cultural interest, be it books, film, comedy, theatre, dance or visiting art galleries. We know they value ethics, as we do. We find that they are drawn to authenticity as well as comfort and practicality. They also like technology. So they like Apple as a brand, but they also value artisanal craftsmanship and quality.

So what things do your potential customers have in common?

Exercise 8

Think hard about the sort of customers who might want to buy your pieces. In your notebook, answer the following twelve questions to describe some imaginary individual customers. It is a good idea to do this at least ten times for different customers.

Questions to fill in each time:

1. What is your customer's name?

2. Draw them or find an image of what they look like.

3. How old are they?

4. Where do they live?

5. What do they do for a living?

6. Roughly how much do they earn?

7. What do they do on weeknights?

8. What do they do at weekends?

9. What media do they engage with (e.g. newspapers, social networks, blogs etc.)?

10. Where do they shop?

11. What makes this customer distinctive from other people?

12. Why do they want your product?

Example

1. **What is your customer's name?**
   Miles

2. **Draw them or find an image of what they look like.**

3. **How old are they?**
   30

4. **Where do they live?**
   Queens Park

5. **What do they do for a living?**
   Architect

6. **How much do they earn?**
   £33,000

7. **What do they do on weeknights?**
   Eat out, visit gym, drinks with friends, dinner parties, gallery openings

8. **What do they do at weekends?**
   Visit friends in the country, go on city-breaks abroad, art galleries, cinema, festivals

9. **What media do they engage with (e.g. newspapers, social networks, blogs etc.)?**
   News online, Instagram, podcasts, Radio 6, blogs, trade magazines (online and hard copy), newspapers occasionally, hates Facebook

10. **Where do they shop?**
    Food - Waitrose and M&S; clothing - occasionally vintage, upcycled brands, Paul Smith, occasionally Ted Baker. Undiscovered eclectic brands and designers.

11. **What makes this customer distinctive from other people?**
    Quite affluent and creative; well educated; lots of culture. Young and probably single.

12. **Why do they want your product?**
    Because they like beautiful things which are ethically sourced and they enjoy discovering new designers. Because my big idea is completely different from what they can already find because . . .

Now List as many different customer types as you can think of who might like your big idea.

Exercise 9

Look through your ten or more imaginary customers carefully and try to summarise them by thinking about what they have in common or giving lower and upper ranges:

- Age range
- Geographical location
- Occupations
- Income brackets
- Common leisure interests
- Media channels

- Shops
- Common attitudes (e.g. to technology or to art)
- Common themes
- Common reasons for wanting your product

Exercise 10

Now that you have a good visualisation of the sort of people who you think would be your customers from Exercises 8 and 9, find some of these types as 'real' people.

Go to these potential customers (at least twenty) and talk to them about your business idea. Don't choose friends and ideally choose complete strangers. Try to persuade them to be honest. Go out in the street with a clipboard if necessary! You might want to offer a prize draw or another incentive like buying them a free coffee to entice them to spend ten minutes with you answering your questions.

Fill in the questions from exercise 8 as well as other questions specific to your offering. For example, you might ask: 'Do you like the idea of buying a hand-made gift for a friend?' or 'Where and when do you shop for gifts and how much do you typically spend?' etc.

Don't overwhelm them with too many questions – ten questions is a good rule of thumb. Remember to listen carefully to what they say and be honest with yourself about their answers.

The exercises in this chapter should have taught you a lot about your market and your potential customers. You may need to repeat this set of exercises several times as you learn from the outcomes. For example, you may find that your first set of research reveals that you were wrong about your offering or about your customers, so you will need to change these things and cycle around again. Do this until you are satisfied that your idea addresses a real market need and also that you understand who the customers are who will actually buy your offering.

Only when you understand your potential market can you work out how to reach those particular types of individuals and let them know about your products. Then you can look for the common threads between potential customers so that you can draw them together and begin to find a way to show them all what you do.

6

Reaching Your Customers

There are *so* many different ways to reach your customers. Once you know who your clients are and what they do, gaining access to them can be a lot easier. For example, if you find that your particular type of customer loves Facebook or eats at a particular type of restaurant, perhaps these might be good ways to connect with them.

You might want to wholesale your pieces to shops where they will mark them up to a higher price and sell them. You might prefer to work directly with clients from your local area or go out and display your wares at exhibitions or other events. Perhaps you'd like to sell them via Etsy, Net-a-Porter or Not On The High Street? There are lots of other ways to spread the word about your offerings, too, that you should perhaps also consider.

If you have discovered through your research so far that your customers really like eating out, perhaps you might do some kind of deal with local restaurants where you give them something when they recommend a customer. For example, you might give their customer a 5 per cent discount if they buy your products (which makes them look good to their customer). Or perhaps you'll make the restaurant owner a gift that they can keep or sell every time they successfully recommend somebody to you.

In my experience, it is often good to see if you can think innovatively here. There will be many tried and tested routes to your market but, perhaps, there is also a completely different way to find new clients. Again, you can use your creativity to think of new ways. Also, technology doesn't stand still for a moment; there is always some new network to tap into.

This chapter runs through some of the well-trodden paths to connect with your market, and in the case studies you will discover some of the routes that other creative people have successfully used. As you will see, it is often a combination of methods that works best, but there is often one of these methods in each case study that is the most effective.

Trade shows

Even if you don't think this is the right way for you to sell your work, visiting the major trade shows in your field can be extremely useful and will help you understand the industry and keep an eye on what everybody else is doing. Most trade shows offer interesting seminar programmes on everything from starting up to spotting the next key trends and these are usually free once you have paid to get in. You will also find a good representation of key industry bodies. You can easily talk to any relevant trade associations or membership groups that seem appealing and they will be able to tell you about any interesting training courses, advice workshops, mentorship programmes or membership packages. Simply chatting to these associations about your plans to start up can be very helpful and they might even offer you a little free advice or connect you with somebody relevant.

If you know you want to sell this way, it is best to visit a trade show first before you exhibit so that you can fully understand how they work, where to site your stand position, and to talk to other exhibitors and pick up some tips. In my experience, most exhibitors are very friendly and helpful to start-ups who smile and ask questions.

Trade shows can be expensive for exhibitors but some offer special rates for first-time exhibitors and it is always worth trying to negotiate on the rate they initially propose. Some trade associations have arrangements with key trade shows so that they can offer discounted show spaces to their members, so it is also worth checking this out. There are also sometimes competitions for new businesses to win free or discounted spaces in special areas for new exhibitors, so these are worth looking out for.

In general, trade shows are not as well visited as they were in the past, perhaps because of the Internet. However, they are still a great way to connect you to buyers and to the industry. This does also mean that the show organisers are often more open to negotiation on the cost of the spaces than they used to be.

Although key buyers always visit the larger trade shows, the ones from larger stores don't always order from start-ups straight away. They want to make sure you actually have a proper supply chain in place and can really deliver before they put in large orders, because they see hundreds of start-ups come and go and can't afford to risk relying on an order that never arrives. However, you might often get orders from smaller retailers and perhaps smaller 'trial' orders from well-known buyers at these first few shows, which help steer you in the right direction and give you some experience. If you fulfil on these reliably, they may well risk a larger order next time.

The following case studies show examples of businesses that have found trade shows to be a particularly successful route to market.

Case Study

The artist Rosemary Goodenough finds that trade shows and collaborations are a good route to market for her business.

When Rosemary was ready to approach the fashion market with her scarves, a contact advised exhibiting at the SCOOP International Fashion Show. She exhibited and then got a letter from London Fashion Week telling her that she had been accepted, even though she hadn't actually applied. She took this as a good sign and decided to attend. Doing those first two trade shows didn't feel scary for Rosemary, who felt instinctively that she was in the right place.

Paul Alger, International Director of the UK Fashion and Textile

Association approached Rosemary at London Fashion Week, suggesting that they collaborate. Rosemary found that membership of the association meant her brand was taken more seriously by buyers, as well as providing her with some excellent advice and invitations to useful talks.

However glamorous a fashion brand is, and however large or small, capturing press attention and buyers at the core shows is critical; all buying is done at trade shows like London Fashion Week, Paris, Milan and New York. Rosemary had been told that it would take four years of exhibiting at trade shows to be seen as a serious contender, but hoped it wouldn't take that long. During the first year, buyers were interested and took her contact details; during the second year they checked to see if she was still there and started asking about her supply chain; then, after three or four years, they finally started placing bigger orders.

'It is very important to be nice to people at trade shows,' advises Rosemary. 'You never know who you are talking to and sometimes even really young bloggers have a huge influence. Some of them are really professional and others can be hard to spot.' Rosemary also met an important broadsheet fashion editor at London Fashion Week who was impressed with her manner when he overheard her chatting to a seventeen-year-old blogger. After this, they became friends and he has become a helpful adviser. 'It is all about listening,' she says.

Case Study

KEITH BRYMER JONES

The ceramicist, Keith Brymer Jones, found that trade shows helped him break into the market.

Keith found that as a creative business making ceramics, it was essential to do trade fairs to get picked up by retailers. However, he suggests choosing the trade shows wisely. 'There are so many different genres of trade show – home, gift, fashion or design. You want to make sure you choose the right one for your market. In my experience, some of the design trade fairs are really good, particularly 100% Design, and Design Week in London is also really good, as is the Shoreditch Design Show.'

Indeed, you have to choose carefully to make sure that you make at least what you spend on your stand and all associated costs. When you are starting out, you can often get funding to show your products from organisations like the Crafts Council or The Prince's Trust. They have special sections in the major trade shows and these can give a great leg-up to new creative businesses. In fact, Keith confided that he himself usually makes a bee-line for these areas now when he is looking for new designers to work with.

Sometimes, if you are in a specific market, there are other more general kinds of trade shows to consider, such as giftware shows, speciality food shows and wedding fairs.

Case Study

Wedding fairs and collaborating are good routes to market for photographer Steve Shipman.

When Steve started up, he began by doing two big national wedding shows each year and a few local wedding fairs, too. The national ones in particular were a huge investment at about £3,000–£4,000 a time. However, they were very successful and helped him build his business, more than paying for themselves each time. He continued with that pattern for about eight years. Now with an established creative business, he no longer finds that he needs to do these events to bring in business as the work comes to him much more easily.

Steve found the fairs very competitive and learned that you need to make your space stand out from the crowd and emphasise how you are different. He says, 'It can become a bit of a price war if there are too many photographers at one fair. For my business, I stick to my prices and stay confident in the value that I can bring. I've seen photographers go out of business by dropping their prices and then they can't actually make it work. So you do need to be careful not to be drawn into all that.'

He occasionally still exhibits at wedding fairs at venues where they recommend him, to help build relationships. Steve finds strong connections with venues make a huge amount of difference to his business. Like most successful creative entrepreneurs, he is also great believer in being kind and respectful to everybody.

Steve also cultivates good relationships with others in the wedding business and remembers the details of good people he works with, like florists or dress designers. He then tries to be as generous as he can with his pictures because letting them have a good picture of their dress is a nice gesture, it will help their marketing, and also encourages them to remember Steve to their clients. He recommends people and they recommend him, too. Wedding fairs are a good way to begin such connections.

At the main jewellery industry trade shows, I always chat to new designers who are exhibiting for the first or second time. They often tell me that they aren't worried that they haven't got any orders yet because other exhibitors tell them that buyers don't always buy at the shows these days, but they might take contact details and order later. I am not sure that this is often true, though, as I do frequently see people placing smaller orders from really good start-ups at jewellery trade shows. So if you finish your first trade show without any orders whatsoever, look at your collection and try to think about how you can improve it or make it more appealing to buyers, as there's every chance that something could be improved.

Website optimising

I speak to a large number of start-ups who still genuinely believe that if you design and build a good website, customers will just automatically come to you via that route. They have no idea that simply having a website means nothing, and you may as well have a lovely showcase of your work in a room somewhere with all of the curtains closed. If nobody can find your website, nobody can buy from it.

Optimising your website is what can make the difference to your site being picked up by search engines and responding to somebody's search. But this is not at all easy. For many years, Tim and I did our own site optimisation but now it is too complicated and we have to use expensive experts to try to keep us towards the top of search engines for the right search phrases.

Having a website and then optimising it on the search engines is no longer a cheap way to market your product or services to the world on its own. You might even have to spend as much successfully marketing a website as you might on renting a shop in your local high street. Generally, the more you spend, the better your page positioning.

If you do decide to try to optimise your website yourself or with the help of professionals, it will take a little time. So don't forget also to advertise your website on your business cards, printed materials and anything that you send to anybody, so that contacts can find you in the meantime while you are still not listed on the search engines.

So if you can't afford to optimise your website, you need to find another way to drive web traffic to the website that you have created. The good news is that there is always another new channel which is free or very cheap (like the Internet was for me years ago). Right now, many businesses are using social networks for this purpose, which can be almost free. You can use your creativity to think of new ways to reach those customers.

Case Study

Social networking and collaborating are good routes to market for photographer Steve Shipman.

When starting out, Steve initially had a bespoke website designed and, of course, created an email address and ensured the details were on everything that he printed or posted. He does quite a lot of Internet marketing, but says that it all starts from his website. He makes sure that he keeps it up to date with his pictures and blogs and then, as he generates more website content, he posts on Facebook or Twitter about those updates. He thinks of this as an important 'constant drip', saying, 'Sharing stuff online works really well – like a shot from a current wedding, for example – but you do need to make sure the client is happy about this, of course.' Steve also really likes Instagram and has been experimenting recently posting some more personal shots.

Start-ups often think that they can just develop a website and then orders will come rushing in. However, you actually have to work very hard driving Internet traffic to your site. So, like many other successful creative business owners, Steve spends time getting his website right and then a lot more time driving traffic to it in various ways.

Twenty years ago, when I started my business, I discovered that the Internet could be a new route to market and worked hard trying to establish how to optimise my website so that it appeared on the first page for the right search-engine search results.

In the 1990s, not many people were using the Internet. However, I knew my way around it a bit because I had been working in the IT industry. Since about 1996–7, I had a very simple web page with one photograph of my jewellery and my contact details, explaining that my speciality was designing and making bespoke jewellery. This site wasn't visited very much and most of my customers came to me because they had been recommended by friends. I'm pretty sure that I was the first jeweller with a website as I couldn't find any others.

One Thursday, I had a call from a young lady in Scotland who had been let down by a shop and wanted a tiara for her wedding on Saturday and a friend had recommended me. In order to meet her tight deadline, I needed to show this customer some pictures of tiara options, as there wasn't time for me to post them to her – you couldn't attach pictures to emails back then and email wasn't used much anyway! So I asked her if she had heard of this thing called 'the Internet'. She said that she thought her friend's geeky brother had this 'Internet' thing on his computer for work. So I explained that I would put some design sketches on my site and she could rush round to his house, dial up to connect, then look at them and instantly choose what she'd like me to make. That way, there would just be time for me to make her choice and still get it to her in the post. This all worked very well and was significantly faster than using the Royal Mail for this kind of communication, so I discovered that this was quite a useful way to show customers pictures without them having to come to see me if they lived miles away. I thought to myself, This Internet thing is quite handy and might just catch on.

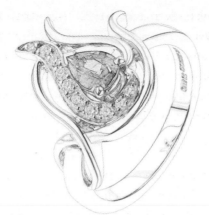

I realised that although this customer had come to me via word of mouth, I could also use the Internet to advertise my jewellery commission service to other people and to help those recommending me to pass on my details.

At first, hardly anybody was using the Internet but, by 1998, I'd worked out that you could alter things to get a website to appear higher up on a search engine for a particular kind of search. Everything on the Internet was very new and there weren't that many websites or search engines, so this wasn't widely understood. I discovered that you could optimise your website by using things called 'meta tags' which would help search engines know whether your site might be relevant for somebody's search; relevant content and appropriate links were useful to improve your positioning, too. I tinkered with these things and soon began to get a lot more enquiries from people who had found me when searching online.

I worked on this over the coming years and, over time, I taught my husband, Tim, how to do this, too. He did a great job and improved the website significantly. It was great working with Tim on this because he didn't know much about jewellery and so just approached the work as though he was a customer. He was always good at imagining what somebody like him would like to see when looking for some jewellery.

Tim was soon outgrowing what Microsoft Publisher could achieve and wanting to do different things and so I bought him a book on how to program in HTML and explained a few of the basics. Over the next few years, he gradually took more and more responsibility for the design and optimisation of my website whenever he was between projects at his own work and able to spend a little time on it. He never looked back and continues to have an innovative attitude towards websites, seeing them as part of the customer experience at every step. Many years later, he is now the managing director of my company.

Social networking

Social networks are well known to be a great way to connect with your market and drive Internet traffic to your website. There is more information about this in Chapter 11 on marketing, but they can also be a good way to experiment with connecting with your market early on, too. You can also easily follow successful creatives on social media and see how they make it work. The next two case studies showcase businesses that rely heavily on social networks as a route to market.

I have noticed that there has been a gradual change in what people want from the social networks of companies and authenticity is high on their wish list. I find that people are often now drawn towards businesses which show their human side on their social networks. Potential clients like to see something of the personalities of a creative individual or team and it helps them decide whether those individuals are people that they might respect or enjoy working with.

Case Study

Laura Sparling uses social networking as her main communication channel for her lampwork beads business.

At first, Laura used to write a blog about her work every day but now she uses Facebook in the same way instead. Her posts are not all about the business as she also injects personality. Laura says, 'I know it sounds a bit cheesy, but I know that my customers aren't just buying my beads or my artwork. They are also buying the story of each little creation and a little bit of me. I think the golden rule with social networking is just to be yourself.'

Laura also urges creatives to be honest about what they are doing. 'Don't put across some kind of persona; I never use the third person because that is really weird. It makes me cringe when I see sole trader artists talking as though they are a whole team. I think you should be proud that you do everything in the business yourself. Customers like that, too.'

Laura regularly posts videos of herself creating beads on her social networking pages. 'For some reason, I stayed away from Facebook for years but now I wish I had been on there sooner. I get loads of business through it, especially now that the videos auto-play on your timeline. This means that people are sucked into watching and then just can't resist clicking on my website and often end up buying my work.' Laura also finds Twitter and Instagram helpful.

More recently, she has begun trying to video the projects that she is particularly enjoying to give them an extra sales boost. This is really working and she finds that her Facebook followers also like to share her videos, bringing even more customers. She adds, 'You can't always predict what people will like. Last year, I made a hedgehog bead just for a laugh and people went crazy for it, which was a big surprise. I had £350 worth of orders for them within minutes – it was so funny and surprising!'

Social networks allow Laura to see very quickly what her customers like, so she can respond to her market and solicit opinions from her followers.

Case Study

Kelly Swallow designs and makes unique patchwork chairs and seating, and also uses social networking as her main route to market.

I first came across Kelly's business many years ago on Twitter. Back then she and I had a few hundred followers. However, Kelly harnessed the power of Twitter as her main marketing tool and now has more than 36,000 followers. The fact that this quantity have signed up to see every tweet that she posts is amazing and means that every time Kelly has a new *product or something to say, a huge number of potential customers instantly see her messages. This has all been completely free to her except, of course, for the time she spends tweeting.*

When Kelly turned her hobby into a creative business, she realised that she should have a website, but this felt like a huge step at the time as she didn't know how to start. Happily, a friend of a friend with a passion for vintage, mid-century furniture kindly developed her website as a favour. Once they had a great website, Kelly and her husband Michael started trying to outdo each other on social media, holding silly competitions about who could get the first interiors blog post somewhere. They tried various social networks like Twitter, Facebook and LinkedIn. From their combined efforts on these three social networks, they managed to get Kelly's chairs on some TV programmes, such as DIY SOS. They also managed to connect with somebody from the luxury home and lifestyle online retailer, Achica, and later from Casafina, which led to great exposure for Kelly's work.

Kelly cites Twitter as by far the best social media platform for her, having built up loads of followers. She and Michael see this as a means of recruiting positive advocates for their brand and products. Twitter and their other social networks drive traffic to her website, which has meant that she hasn't had to do very much search-engine optimisation at all. 'Only a few years ago, it wouldn't have been possible for a company like mine to have customers in Australia, but now we have, simply because of the power of social networks and the Internet.'

Collaborating with other like-minded businesses

Many creatives find that collaborating with other like-minded businesses can open up new markets for them. Sometimes, this can be in the form of reciprocal recommendations (and we've already seen that Steve Shipman finds this way of working useful in the earlier case study).

I have noticed that some businesses have been finding ever more interesting and inventive ways of doing this. For example, on the tables of a good restaurant I recently noticed they were recommending a high-end local baking course. And a while ago, a local restaurant which happens to be owned by some of our lovely customers invented a cocktail named the 'HK Bespoke' for us.

The right kind of collaboration will bring something to each party that they could not have found alone.

Case Study

22ct GOLD GUILT 19g TOP

OLIVE CUT

HAND BLOW CRYSTAL BOTTLE.

Mohammed Jamal, the London perfumer, had found selling his product through conventional perfume outlets was not the right model for him.

Mohammed went on a long journey through conventional perfume shops and then decided that the mainstream retail model was not right for his perfumery business. Over time, he worked out that collaborations with artisans or well-connected individuals to target individual bespoke clients are the best route to market for what he has to offer. He was surprised to discover that, for him, perfumery does not need to be all about retail. Actually, he has always been driven by wanting to give people an experience of perfumery rather than just to sell one product. He helps individuals experience how perfumes are made and works with them to create their perfect bespoke scents.

'The business environment in which I was growing up, training in and working with was all telling me that perfumery has to be offered via the conventional tools of mass retail, marketing and PR. Those same tools

became barriers, because I believed that the only way to achieve my vision was through those channels.

'It is only much more recently that I realised that I must believe in myself and not actually depend on these conventional channels. So I now work on products and experiences that are about one-to-one interaction with a strong educational and bespoke element. I don't need a large retail environment for this. Instead, I am collaborating with other like-minded businesses who are dealing with international clients on a one-to-one basis in a similar way, ensuring that we have shared values and vision. While I still offer off-the-shelf, retailed scents, too, this is an entry level to introduce the core bespoke experience offering.'

Wholesaling

A traditional route to market for creatives is to sell to other retailers, and this is called 'wholesaling', even when you stock them with one-offs and small quantities. However, you have to be prepared to accept some fairly hefty mark-ups. Most large retailers expect to mark up your pieces about two-and-a-half times before they sell them. So if you make something and sell it to them for £50, they will expect to sell it in the £100-£125 area. Many start-ups are horrified by this when they first learn that the shops often make more on their products than they do. However, don't forget that it also often costs them more to sell your products than it takes you to make them. This margin is how they pay their extremely high rent, rates, insurance, VAT and staff salaries, and also make a profit themselves. Some smaller or less well-known stores or galleries might accept a smaller margin.

In addition to the high margins, some retailers ask newer designers to give them their items on 'sale or return', which means that you lend them your pieces but you don't get a penny for them unless they sell. If they don't sell after a certain time period, then they'll give them back to you; so you take all of the risk. So you need to weigh up carefully whether this kind of business model will work for you.

In my experience, not all shops look after your products well and, occasionally, I have found that they have allowed my pieces to be damaged or scratched through careless handling. Some galleries and boutiques who work this way are less committed to selling your work than they would be if they had bought the items from you. You need to keep an eye on them as your creations might disappear into a stock room and be forgotten, or they might not be displayed to their best advantage, kept clean or properly lit. Many creatives who rely on selling in this way like to visit the stores and galleries regularly to clean, tidy and check their stock.

However, despite all of this, most creatives find that selling through a shop or gallery can still work well for them as a route to market and to help them establish and grow their brand presence.

Case Study

Celia Hart, the illustrator and print maker, uses galleries, shops and social networking as her route to market.

As Celia's business took off, she started exhibiting her lino prints in a couple of small local galleries, which took a 30 per cent commission. Then, other gallery owners saw her work and asked her to exhibit with them. Celia found that when she went into these larger galleries, she had to put up her prices considerably because their required commissions were more like 60 per cent.

All of her work has to be lent to galleries on a 'sale or return' basis, so Celia has to pay for the cost of framing, and essentially takes all of the risk herself.

Celia finds that because of the high commissions taken by the galleries, she only just breaks even on some of her framed prints. Despite this, Celia says that it is definitely worth it. Country Living *approached her after seeing her work in a gallery and this was an important publicity step for her, which led to work with design and product branding agencies. One Cambridge gallery, in particular, has been a brilliant marketing tool for her as so many creative and interesting people go there. She is regularly approached about other illustration work as a result.*

The sale-or-return model used to be a particular problem with Celia's greetings cards because she would find that they would send back any unsold cards with their gallery price stickers still attached. This resulted in her having to repackage them at her own expense which wasted a lot of time and money, so she no longer sells cards on sale or return. Now, starting with a small initial order, galleries and gift shops buy her cards at the trade price and these sales then cover the production cost of the cards. The trade sales of cards helps Celia cover the cost of delivering sale-or-return framed prints to the galleries.

If you do the maths and can sell enough volume, wholesaling to other retailers can work extremely well, and it is a good way to get your products 'out there'. If you manage to get your work into successful shops and make good relationships, then this way of working enables you to concentrate on creating while they focus on the display, selling and even sometimes marketing for you. The right relationship with the right store can turn you from an unknown into a household name. As you will see in the case study below, Keith Brymer Jones found that relationships are absolutely key to successful wholesaling.

Sometimes, it can be very hard to get your foot in the door and even just to show your items to buyers. However, there is always a way and, if luck is on your side, you'll find you can get your work in front of the right person at the right time.

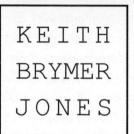

KEITH BRYMER JONES

Keith Brymer Jones found that trade shows and approaching retailers directly worked well for his ceramics business and helped him break into the market.

Keith managed to get his work into stores even before doing any trade shows. He had been trained to throw hundreds or even thousands of pots quite quickly, so figured that he could cope with supplying shops on his own. 'Entirely out of my own vanity, I devised my own range of pots and took a couple of them into Heal's, the London homeware store on Tottenham Court Road. I left them on the front desk and was quite lucky because they did get shown to their ceramics buyer.' Shortly afterwards, the buyer phoned Keith saying she liked his work and invited him to make some pieces for Heal's. 'I only really went there because it was on my bus route – I didn't really expect to pull it off!'

At first, Heal's ordered a total of 50–100 pots from Keith at a time in various shapes. They did well, so the order increased to 200 of each design the next time. Heal's stocked this same range as he grew it for about four years, which worked well. This experience showed him how the whole system works with buyers. It was the late 1980s and early 1990s and stores were only just becoming involved in fashion-centred interiors, so this was a whole new area. They liked working with Keith because he was happy to come in and look at their mood boards, go away and design something exclusively for them for that season and make enough pots to cater for the store. Then he could design and make something new and fresh in the same way the following season. Keith found that being a small business meant that he could be really flexible in his approach, which satisfied his customer's requirements at the time.

Over the following years, Keith managed to win many other clients on the high street like Habitat, Monsoon and Laura Ashley. This was partly because a couple of the buyers he'd been working with at Heal's moved jobs into those other stores and they then signed him up because they had found that he fulfilled orders and was easy to work with. He was soon throwing about 800–1,000 pots every day and working long hours. Next, he was approached by Conran to stock their stores and a whole spectrum of buyers wanted his work after that.

One thing that Keith had to get used to was selling his own work and he still struggles with this because he feels such an emotional attachment to it. 'You can get so excited about people liking it that you say "yes" to everything, including the low price they suggest! Once you know the kind of prices that the stores need to pay, you need to stand your ground, really, because buyers will always try to negotiate.' Keith advises that creatives should get somebody else to sell their work if possible, even just a friend on commission. He finds this is really effective, saying, 'They can big up your work for you, even if you aren't confident enough to do this yourself.'

At one stage, he realised that he was doing larger runs than ever, about 10,000–15,000 pots per contract, but when he looked at the figures he realised that he had priced some of these pieces too low and was losing money. So he learned not to let his price slip too low after that. 'When you are negotiating, remember that a deal is only a good deal if both parties are happy. There are too many times that I've walked out of a meeting feeling uncomfortable about what I've agreed to.'

Keith advises, 'The Apprentice show is all about hard-hitting sales-speak, but real negotiations shouldn't be like that. You definitely shouldn't screw over your clients for all they've got. This is an awful way to live your life and doesn't help you.'

I agree wholeheartedly; if you work out a deal that works for everybody in a friendly, amicable manner, you are likely to get future business from that client and the relationship will be far better for your business in the long run.

Now that Keith works with manufacturers and suppliers all over the world, he still works by this adage and makes sure that he isn't always trying to drive the hardest deal possible. In fact, he recently offered an additional 10 cents per piece to his main suppliers. 'They couldn't believe it in the factories, but we believe in doing the right thing and that being nice to work with is key. Then they won't feel hard done by and I think we get better quality out of them as a result, too.'

It is still worth just taking your work to retailers to see if they'd like to sell your products. You never know, you might get lucky and be in on the same day as the buyer. If you are nice to the sales staff, they might even tell you when the buyer is due to visit. It is worth being very persistent and pursuing the buyers to give you feedback on your samples relentlessly, as Anna discovered in the next case study.

While I agree with Keith that you must be careful not to let your price drop too low, when you are working in higher volumes and starting out, you might have to do a few jobs at pretty tight margins to show buyers that your products really can sell and that you really can deliver. Then you can gradually nudge up your prices when the retailer has seen the demand.

What I think is crucial to Keith's success story is that he made himself ideal to work with; he adapted to work in the way that satisfied his buyers – he thought about what his clients wanted and then fitted his business offering around that. He made sure that he always fulfilled his orders and was very professional in his approach to work. When you are nice to everybody and easy to work with, then people are quick to want to work with you again and to recommend you.

Many designers also manage to break into international wholesale markets, like Anna in the next case study.

Case Study

Anna Scholz found success for her exclusive plus-size fashion brand through persistence when wholesaling to various top retailers, but is now focusing on 'direct e-tailing'.

When starting out, Anna made herself a list of 200 stores where she'd like to sell her collections. She narrowed this down to a 'gold list' of 25 stores she very strongly wanted to stock, before researching and trying to discover the names of the buyers, which can be difficult and time-consuming. Anna targeted her 'gold list' relentlessly, first sending each a package via UPS, suspecting that while ordinary post would be opened by an assistant, a beautifully presented package from a courier was unlikely to be ignored. She followed the parcels up with phone calls and was very persistent, 'Some of these buyers needed a lot of time . . . sometimes it took a year or more before I managed to get into their stores.' She laughs, 'I did also do one naughty thing, which was that I got all of my girlfriends to call Harrods and ask for my collection so that they noticed a "demand". It did work eventually, but took a very long time!'

Anna found building up contacts in America was particularly challenging. Fairly early on, she took a business trip to America with her collection. She made loads of appointments with New York buyers and had hired an expensive hotel room because it had the right lighting to display the clothes. On the first day, every single one of her appointments either cancelled or didn't turn up.

On another occasion, Anna's entire collection got stuck in Customs and so she had to turn up to her appointments with buyers without the clothes that she had gone there to show. Each time, she learned from these challenges and kept persisting. Once she got into the top stores, she then discovered that buyers move jobs a lot in the USA and sometimes a new buyer wants to mark their arrival by ditching lots of previous brands. So you can be in one minute, and out the next.

Anna also found international trade shows useful and says that the British Fashion Council has a lot of schemes to support British businesses who want to find a global audience. 'They give something like half of the cost of the travelling and trade show expenses for the first two seasons. I tried out different markets like that, which was really useful. I always believed strongly in going international and I think that some fashion designers can think in too insular a way. I was keen to go to places like Paris, Milan, Denmark and the USA to discover where I could pick up the best buyers.'

After much persistence, Anna managed to have her collections accepted into many well-known stores including Harrods, Selfridges and Bloomingdale's and this route to market worked very well for her for many years.

However, a few years ago, many of the big stores started to close their plus-size departments and move those collections online. This caused Anna's company all sorts of problems. For example, a big online retailer put a promotion on to their website where their lines were 20 per cent off on a particular weekend, which then affected smaller retailers badly. These price differences also led to customers trying things on in store and then ordering online where they can get a better price. Anna has had problems when some larger retailers want items to go on sale earlier than Anna is comfortable with. 'You end up watching some kind of price war and it is all a bit of a mess,' she says. So, in 2016, she changed to be the exclusive e-tailer of her own collections and will no longer be wholesaling. Anna says, 'It was a little scary at first, but we quickly built up a lot of online traffic and, of course, mark-ups have increased, because we are retailing directly ourselves which makes a big difference.'

So Anna's marketing emphasis now is on driving traffic to her own website, and they have a digital marketing company who do search-engine optimisation to drive traffic to them. They are doing quite a bit of Facebook advertising, which they find works quite well, because they can target a very specific market.

Anna is also looking at some interesting collaborations with some well-known companies in Germany, America and in the UK. Anna says, 'These collaborations are very exciting because they don't only create sales, but they also make many more people aware of your brand because they are pushing your name out there, which leads to lots of brand recognition.'

I also tried wholesaling for my own jewellery business, and then pulled out of it. However, I still think that this stage was important for my business and for me as a designer, trying to learn how I might fit into the jewellery industry.

Back in 1998–9, when I was still trying to refine the direction of my business, I decided that I wanted to get my jewellery into a really good London store. I had always admired Liberty and loved learning about the ideas that led to the founding of the store during design history classes at university. So I decided to be brave and approach them to see if they might be interested in stocking my jewellery.

I took some tiaras that I had made and caught the train to London without calling ahead. I did this on purpose because it seemed to be impossible to get on the phone to a major buyer and so I wanted to try just turning up.

I was very lucky because, that day, when I went up to their beautiful bridal department, the buyer was there and agreed to see me for ten minutes. She was a very elegant lady called Joanne and we got on instantly. Her department was beautiful and I felt as though I might be sitting in a heavenly cloud of ivory furniture and carpets, showering her with my sparkling samples.

Joanne liked my tiaras straight away and they were rather different from the other three designers that they stocked. She also loved that I could provide a level of customisation and explained that she felt her customers would really value that. She chose six of my designs to stock and asked me to provide her with colour and texture samples for the different finishes and options that I could provide. I could even get pearly beads dyed to match a bride's wedding dress which she liked, too. Before I knew what was happening, my jewellery was on sale in the beautiful cabinets of Liberty.

I was so proud to have my jewellery in Liberty and I felt that something was really beginning to work. I had always admired the business and it felt so empowering to be part of this institution that had been supporting good quality design for so many years.

Over the next couple of years, Liberty sold quite a few of my tiaras and I added some new designs, hair clips, Alice bands, matching pendants and earrings and these sold well, too. When I mentioned that I mainly made bespoke fine jewellery, Joanne asked me to design and make her own engagement ring which was a huge compliment, considering that she could have asked absolutely anybody, and it was the biggest project I had done at the time.

Back then, Liberty was not good at paying their suppliers. It was hard work for designers like me because we had to take all of the risk ourselves by providing all of our samples on a 'sale or return' basis. Liberty has changed a lot since then and is under completely new management, and I gather they look after their designers very well these days. But then when they sold my work, they took absolutely ages to pay – some payments didn't reach me for six months. I continually had to phone their accounts department chasing cheques.

They also, like all retailers, took my prices and multiplied them by 2.75 or 3 in order to set their retail price. So I would sell them an Alice band for £50 and they'd sell it for £140–£150. I might not see that £50 until six or seven months after I had delivered it and, of course, I had already paid for the materials prior to that.

After a couple of years of working this way, Joanne called me and told me that she had some really bad news. Liberty Bridal Wear was going to merge into another department and was closing down. I'm still not exactly sure what happened, as every time I went in there it was full of brides ordering dresses and appeared to be running well, but she explained that it was all terrible and some of the wedding dress designers who were owed thousands or tens of thousands of pounds were unlikely to be paid at all. At the time, I was owed about £400 and was terrified that it might not be paid. Joanne herself was going to have to leave because the whole department was closing. Other departments were restructuring, too. Despite her personal worries, Joanne was extremely kind and told me that she was going to fight my corner and try to ensure that I was paid as one of the smallest businesses they were working with. Sure enough, my cheque arrived in the post a couple of weeks later, thank goodness.

By this time, I also had my jewellery in two other exclusive designer stores run by friends. So while I had only approached Liberty by then, I found myself with a separate wholesale arm to the business. It was such hard work keeping just these three happy and chasing payments that I couldn't imagine what a nightmare it might be stocking, say, forty different retailers who also might not be so friendly. The prices had to be so low for them to take a realistic margin that I was working hard for little gain.

I gradually extracted myself from these arrangements and decided that I should stick to working with my customers directly, being the designer, the manufacturer and also the retailer. Only then could I be really sure that customers were getting the very best service and being presented with all of the options in a way that I could manage.

However, I never lost the confidence that selling my jewellery in Liberty had given me and it was a great stepping stone towards success. So I have always been extremely grateful for their recognition.

Finding an audience

In Chapter 5, we looked at how to work out your customer type. If you have identified that your particular type of customer visits a certain type of venue regularly, then it makes sense that you might want your product to be on show there. For example, you might have noticed that your customer types visit theatres or particular restaurants or other venues. You could think about lending the venue some of your work to show free of charge, to see if you can develop enquiries that way. I have noticed a lot of artists working this way, even on a small scale, by exhibiting on the walls of well-established art cafés and I gather it can work well. However, I have also been to such establishments where the art was not displayed well and was dusty, clearly not selling very often. My advice is to try to think bigger and more inventively or it might be a waste of time. Where's a really good place to showcase your work that would impress your particular customer type?

As you read earlier, Dominic and Frances from Scabetti found that having their installations in high-profile locations, like Jill and Rick Stein's restaurant and also in the IMO's headquarters in London, led to many other commissions and sales. Frances says that once a piece is somewhere high-profile, your skills are endorsed and it gives others the confidence to approach you and naturally generates sales.

There are so many routes to market, and sometimes I notice that business comes to us from very unexpected sources. For example, I recently spotted an unexpected altruistic route to market. I am often asked to do talks for charity groups about Fairtrade gold, recycling old jewellery or about starting a creative business. I am always happy to say 'yes' when I can – after all, for me there really isn't anything more important in life than trying your best to be good to others and attempting to make the world a tiny bit better through what you do. It was then pointed out to me recently that quite regularly some of the audience at those events who had not previously heard of us then became our customers. So I learned that sometimes routes to market can come from unexpected places. This certainly isn't why I do these talks, but is a nice and surprising bonus.

Exercise 11

Write down in order of priority what you think your five best routes to market will be. Think about how you can be sure that those routes to market will work for your particular customer type and write a few bullet points or draw a mind-map about these.

Think about alternative ways to get to the same group of customers. For example, you might want to collaborate with a restaurant at which they eat, be interviewed by a magazine that they read or run an open workshop in a venue they visit.

I find mind-maps quite useful for this kind of thinking and there are loads of great apps and websites that you can use as a tool for these. However, a straight list can work well, too, if it seems better for you. Your answers to Exercise 11 will help to form the foundations of a marketing plan later. Most successful creative business leaders regularly go through this process in one form or another.

Once you have your list of how to get to your market, you can put these steps in order of priority and begin making the right connections to turn your list into reality.

7

Researching Your Competition

So, now that you have your big idea and know who your customers are and how you plan to reach them, you need to check out the competition more thoroughly. Is there anybody else doing anything that closely resembles your offering? You need to research thoroughly anything that might seem similar to your customers, and try to work out whether your niche is strong enough. If not, you might need to tweak your big idea accordingly.

If you sell beautiful, hand-made, crochet baby shawls made from knitted Angora rabbit fur, you need to focus on researching products you think have the most in common with your creations; there is little point in comparing them to lower-quality, imported baby shawls from a supermarket because their customers are in a different market to yours. It might be worth comparing them to high-quality, high-street equivalents though, such as anything from the White Company. You need to think about where your customers might look for shawls or similar gifts.

This chapter will help you through the process of comparing, charting and analysing your competition to see whether your niche is strong enough.

Charting your competitors

Exercise 12

Make a simple chart showing your 5-10 key competitors, noting their price points, what their advantages are, how they reach their customers and any other key features.

Once you've done that, write down what available niches this reveals to you. As you can see from the example below, it helps you to identify clearly what your differences are, and you can then decide if your uniqueness is strong enough.

If there aren't any direct competitors, pick the next best thing - for example, when I started there were no other jewellers who offered a bespoke jewellery design service, so I compared myself to other high-quality independent jewellers selling good-quality, hand-made jewellery.

If your competitors have stores, it is a good idea to be brave and go in pretending to be a potential customer. You can then look at their products and see the quality close up, and also learn a lot about their customer service. Try to include as much detail on this chart as you can.

Example

Competitor Spreadsheet

Company	Retailers	Prices	Advantages	Comments
London Handbag Basics	Amazon, LondonBagBasics.co.uk Sebbenams department store & online.	£50–£80	One handbag, and you change the outer panel only with 8 different colour/pattern options	Interesting concept but quite naff and not very classy options available. Probably not for my market. Plasticky handbag straps. Leopard-skin – yuck!

The Bag Organiser Insert Company	4 big department stores (Sebbenhams, Lewis, Cellidges and Fresias in store and online). TBO.com	£30–£40	One insert you put into any bag you already have.	Quite pricey for what it is, as it isn't actually a bag. Quite a few design problems with this one. Only one option. Hasn't got the pockets you need.
Party Fold-Ups	eBay, Amazon and in some specialist boutiques like Janie's Dress Shops, Powderpuff Blue and Tilley.	£20–£30	Quite stylish fabric pouch which rolls up. Available in lots of different nice fabrics and colours.	Nice but not very practical as they take ages to open up and you can't easily grab stuff from them. Can be used for different uses like make-up brushes or art materials.
Chinese Bag Inserts	eBay, Amazon.	£3–£7	Very cheap. Machine washable. Available in quite a few colours. Good size.	Cheap but do look cheap and so not very classy at all. Colours are a bit over-bright. Only sold online. Take ages to arrive from China. Really low quality.
My Company: Harriet's Handbags	HarrietHandbags.com Hope to approach various boutiques and high-end department stores.	£100–£300	Ethically made. Really high quality. Good designs. Machine washable inserts. You can keep buying new inserts. Different sizes available. Bright and attractive designs. Durable.	Need really classy branding and labelling to command the price and tell the ethics story. Sell to high-end shops.

Once you have completed this chart, you will clearly see how you might fit in. Remember, you are looking for a clear 'gap' for your own offering. You will also be able to understand what you need to charge for your creations in order to be perceived as good value, expensive or cheap to your customers, depending on what you are trying to achieve.

Using a SWOT analysis

If you find that you have a direct competitor who might be too close for comfort, or who you want to examine more closely, you can do a more thorough analysis. Get a piece of paper and divide it into four. In each quarter you write 'Strengths', 'Weaknesses', 'Opportunities' and 'Threats'. This is chart is called a SWOT analysis. This is also a particularly useful exercise for you to apply to your own company, too.

Strengths – here you should list anything that you can think of that is good about the products or company who supply them. It should include anything unique about their products or ranges, any advantages of their products; perhaps they have a lot of experience or a good reputation, a big budget, good quality or competitive prices. Perhaps they are known for good customer service or innovative designs. Do they already have a chain of stores or a good supply network?

Weaknesses – here you list everything that is not so good about the products or company who supply them. What are the gaps in their products or ranges? Is their branding or packaging up to scratch? Do they have a poor reputation for customer service or poor quality? Are they a small company who might have financial difficulties expanding?

Opportunities – what might your competitors do to develop a stronger position? Are there trends in their industry, or consumer trends that might be relevant? Any new technology they might embrace to enhance what they do? Are there external financial factors that might mean people want to spend more on their products? Are other competitors weak, meaning that they might build a stronger position in the future? What about global developments – might they reach overseas markets?

Threats – are there environmental or social issues in their supply chain? Anything political on the horizon that might be a problem for the company or products? Any new technology that might affect them negatively? Is there new government legislation that might negatively affect them by, for example, raising the cost of the raw materials they use? Any economic external or internal issues? Any trends that might cause them problems if they don't keep up?

Exercise 13

Complete a SWOT analysis for your closest competitor. And then run another SWOT analysis for the offering that you are planning.

Example

SWOT chart for my biggest competitor, The Bag Organiser Insert Company

Strengths	Weaknesses
Hard-wearing insert with good design.	Design weakness – Currently only 3 colours, 1 design/size option and a bit small for most day-bags, and too big for evening bags.
They are stocked in at least 4 of the main retailers.	
They seem to be fulfilling their ordering network well as the shops are always well stocked with their products.	Aren't machine washable and fiddly to wipe by hand.
	They are not generally well known or advertised/marketed.
Shop staff say the quality is OK and customers don't complain etc.	
	Shop staff told me they don't sell that often.
	Quite expensive at £30.
	Their packaging and branding is a bit old-fashioned.
	Their designs are not that young or modern so limited appeal.

Opportunities	Threats
They could work on their designs.	Everybody is feeling financial pinch so maybe will spend less on themselves and their handbags.
They could change their branding to bring it up to date.	
	Materials might not be the best.
After Brexit, pound is good value for others so international trade would be good to investigate.	Responsible sourcing? This could become more of an issue over time for them.
They could diversify to other products.	There is no reason for a customer to buy more than one.
	Trends are for bags to get smaller and this may affect them.
	Their idea has been copied online from China very cheaply.

Embracing and refining your difference

Once you have completed the SWOT analysis, you should find that you can more clearly see if this competitor is so close that you want to think again about your idea, or whether you think you can forge ahead regardless.

I find that it is a very good idea to keep a close eye on what other jewellers are doing. However, I never then try to do what they do; instead, it helps keep me brave and keen to ensure that I am always doing something that is confidently different. This gets harder as you become more established, because so many other businesses try to copy you, but it is always possible.

Keith Brymer Jones keeps an eye on his competition, ensuring he isn't swept along by mass trends in the ceramics and homeware sector by staying true to his own creative difference.

Keith has a very interesting take on looking at other ceramics products. He consciously looks at the competition at trade shows and then actively tries not to be influenced by their designs, instead following his own heart.

'There always seems to be some trend or other going round. For example, a few years ago it was Union Jacks and then skulls and, after that, there was a stag fashion. It would be very easy just to decide to do a stag pot that goes along with that, but instead I always try to do exactly the opposite, within reason! I try not to look at company trend analysis reports and the like because, even though those kind of things can be a bit interesting, I think that if you know too much about what is on trend and think too hard about the gap you are going to fill, you can actually end up being less creative. Your work can end up looking too forced and you can lose your spark.'

Keith says he also lives by the rule: 'A pessimist's problem is an optimist's opportunity'. He feels that in every cloud there is a silver lining and all you have to do is to find it.

8

Pricing

The SWOT analysis you have just completed will have told you quite a lot about how things are priced in your market. This will help you to see what kind of prices might be perceived as cheap or expensive by your potential customers and, more importantly, what 'good value' means to your customers. Nobody wants to think that the things they are buying are expensive for no good reason. But your creations can cost quite a bit more than mass-produced brands as long as there is a reason for this that the customer believes is valuable to them. For example, maybe it is hand-made, the quality is great or the materials are extra special or ethically sourced.

This chapter will help you decide how to price your products and includes case studies illustrating how different creatives found their way in this area.

Paying your bills and valuing your time

Choosing a price that feels right for your market is vital but it is also important to think about your pricing the other way round to ensure that your costs are properly covered, otherwise you can end up guessing a price that eventually means that you are not making enough money to pay yourself properly.

I often hear that creatives are advised to double their costs to find their retail price, but I don't always agree with this. If your materials cost £10 and you sell your product for £20, but are likely to only sell a low volume of pieces, this might not make you enough money. This probably won't be enough income from each piece you sell to cover your costs, pay yourself for your time and give you some extra funds with which to grow your business into your vision of success. It isn't as though you are just buying something like a mass-produced product and selling it on without adding value to it with your creativity.

When you are starting out, it is also a good idea to consider an hourly rate that your time is 'worth' and put that into your pricing somewhere. For example, you may decide that your creative energy is worth £20 per hour or, ideally, more, depending on the rarity and value of your skill and the pace of your work.

If you aren't sure how much you should charge per hour for your time, be brave and ask somebody who is already in the business. If they are kind, they will usually tell you how to make a start with this. A lot depends on how fast you work. For example, the reason that goldsmiths' salaries increase as they become more experienced is that they speed up and can do more in the time and also know how to handle increasingly tricky projects.

However, sometimes when you are starting out and get an amazing opportunity, it might even be worth considering undercharging for your time, or even not charging for it at all, in order to get your foot in the door. However, as some of the later case studies found, be careful not to end up being unable to pay your bills or eat!

Working out what you need to charge

Exercise 14

List the following information for each of your products on an individual basis:

- Cost of materials

- Number of hours to make multiplied by my hourly rate

- Any other production costs

- Packaging cost

Add these up and then multiply resulting total by 1.5 for higher-priced materials like leather bags, or 2 for low-cost materials like greetings cards. This multiple will allow for covering overheads and a profit margin.

Example

Using the Angora baby shawl as the imaginary product:

- Cost of materials - £5.50
- Number of hours to make - 2 hours
- My hourly rate - £15 per hour
- Any other production costs £0.25 (label)
- Packaging cost £2

Total = £37.75, so this is the minimum price you should ideally sell for, whether this is wholesale or retail. However, this is not the price I'd suggest selling at - see the continuation of this example later in this chapter.

The price that you come to (the £37.75 in this example) is called your 'cost-based price'. Using this can work particularly well for things that you will be making in higher volumes. Most creatives find that this isn't quite the right price level when they are making in lower volumes; instead, they like to look at cost pricing and value pricing, or look at both and then take a decision between the two. (Value pricing is explained a little later in this chapter.)

As you grow, each item that you sell also has to include a little contribution to your overheads for the business, like rent, rates and insurance, as otherwise there is no way to pay your business bills. You also need to allow an amount for the time spent designing or making your pieces, too, and cover other necessary costs to keep you fed, housed, happy and enthusiastic.

KEITH
BRYMER
JONES

Keith Brymer Jones works in higher volumes and likes to keep his pricing fairly simple.

When Keith used to work out his own pricing, he says, 'I used to do all of the boring stuff like working out how long it will take and my hourly rate and add on materials and everything. Then I would double that figure. That doubling covers your extras like going out to get the coffee or picking up the phone. Then you need to look at what price that gives you. But remember that you can price it higher and then it can come down, but you can never put a price up. So even if you are worried that nobody will pay your doubled price, start off top heavy and then come down if necessary.'

Keith advises that pricing can be tough for creatives to do and that it can work well to get a friend to do this with you to make sure you don't sell your work too cheaply. 'Pricing is important to get right. You can make so much more money [per item], but make sure the price is just right so that you can sell enough volume, too.' This is certainly true – even just a few pence more on a price can make a massive difference when you are working in volume.

Now, Keith and his business partner Dom take on separate roles. Keith designs and makes the pieces and Dom does the numbers. This works really well for Keith as he doesn't always think that numbers are his strength and has a tendency to price his work too cheaply on his own.

This doubling of the cost price would have made a lot of sense for a start-up like Keith's where he makes very high volumes. However, this might not work for a craftsperson who is working on one-off pieces and selling directly to customers, who should instead look at value pricing. Don't forget that here Keith was also selling to a retailer, so he had to be careful not to price too highly because the retailer will also have had to add on their own significant mark-up to pay for their high costs and make a profit. So this price was his wholesale price, not his retail price.

Working out your value price

The earlier pricing exercise shows you what you 'need' to charge and so will give you the minimum price that you could try to sell your item for (wholesale or retail), but is only a 'guesstimate'. Your product should ideally sell for a higher retail price if the customers will pay it and if your items are perceived to be more valuable than this. There are some exceptions to this – for example, if you are using very rare and expensive raw materials like leather or precious metals, you probably won't be able to go as high as a 1.5-multiple mark-up as it may make your product too costly for the customer.

Your actual cost-based price will need to take a more accurate account of your overheads and other variable costs as you grow, but that will become clearer over time. However, the previous exercise will have given you a guide for the moment.

Now ask yourself – is that a realistic retail price? This is where you need to have done your research to get a really good 'feel' for what your customers expect to pay for the combination of quality and product that you are planning to make. This is often rather different from the outcome of your cost-based price calculation. Hopefully, your value price will be higher but, sometimes, it can be lower.

If your cost-based price calculation has given you a price that already seems too high for your market, you might need a big rethink. Check your calculations carefully but, if they are correct, it may be that your product just can't make you enough money to be viable.

If your cost-based price calculation gives you a figure that seems too low, then you should raise it to what feels right for the market. If you don't, then people will make subliminal decisions based on your price and decide it must be lower in quality than other offerings, which will not do you any favours. The price that you come to which feels right for your product, quality and market and is already higher than your cost-based calculation is called your value price.

Remember that, within reason, it is easier to position it at a higher price to start with (you can always come down later, but it is harder to raise it). Be careful, though – you don't want to reduce it so significantly early on that people start to wonder what is going on.

This is where the way to work out your price can feel a bit 'woolly'.

You need to have a feel for what you think your skill and creativity is worth, which is what people will actually pay for it, and up the price that you worked out accordingly.

Case Study

Laura Sparling feels that she has to bring her prices lower than she would ideally like.

She knows what price her beads 'should' be from the amount of time they take to produce, but she doesn't feel that she can sell them at that figure as it feels too high. Sometimes, she wonders if she should write what price they 'should' be to make people realise how much time and care goes into every single one.

To price her work, Laura looks around online and on Etsy to see what others are selling for and then compares their prices and quality to her own work. After that, she thinks about the lowest sale price she would be happy to settle for. 'From that information, I pitch my price at the point that feels about right between the two.'

I personally feel that most of Laura's prices are still too low and may not truly reflect her 'position' in her market (price and positioning is explained later on in this chapter). I think that she should be more confident about what she brings to her brand.

Price points

'Price points' are specific retail price figures that you might use for your creations which have been thought out in order to compete best with the prices of other products.

There are some price points which feel more comfortable to customers than others. It is a strange thing but some retailers find that things that would not sell at £116.50, sell like hot cakes at £125. Also, some things that won't sell at all at £103 sell really well at £99.

I have found that price points have changed a lot over the last twenty years. This is not only because, of course, prices have inevitably gone up, but also because consumer opinion on price points has changed and evolved. Twenty years ago, pretty much every retailer priced at the £xx.99 point routinely whether they were higher or lower end. For example, things might be £4.99 rather than £5, or might be £199, or even £199.99, rather than £200. This really did work, as people do subliminally feel that something below certain thresholds is within reach, but over certain thresholds seems much more expensive, even if this difference is only 1p. It seems crazy and many of us would like to think that this isn't true for us, but we don't even consciously know that we are being guided by our gut on whether something feels within reach or expensive in this way.

These days, I find that 'lower-end' retailers like discount shops or supermarkets are still using the 99p or sometimes 95p price points, but medium- and high-end retailers have changed this. I think this is because there was negative feeling among some customers who became irritated by the 99p or 95p price point – feeling it was manipulative, annoying and somehow inauthentic. These days, authenticity really matters to consumers. Many retailers, therefore, have now completely abandoned this kind of pricing structure and instead price at points like £5.50 or £125. So I have seen that popular price points do change over time.

Have a careful look at price points in shops when you are out and about – especially in shops that your own customers might use. Think about whether they should include pence or not. Think about particular numbers that do and don't work. For example, I find that prices with a 6 in them anywhere don't work in my market and notice that these are almost never used elsewhere, too – I have no idea why! This kind of price point research will help you to ascertain good price points to use for your market.

Price and positioning

Most markets are quite crowded with lots of different products available, which sometimes overlap offering similar benefits. When something is well 'positioned' within its market, it stands out from other products and this allows a brand or company to charge a higher price for it because it has something unique about it. So part of your consideration about pricing needs to be how you think that your price will reflect upon your positioning in the market, because when you choose your price, you are 'saying' something about how you feel it ranks in the order of price and value compared to other brands, which may be more or less expensive.

You may have noticed from your pricing research into your competitors that high-quality brands always price at certain levels and lower ones at cheaper levels. For example, you may notice that certain purses often fall in the £30–£40 range, but there are higher-quality ones at the £100–£120 level. When you look carefully at the differences between the actual products, you may not notice a vast amount of difference. Perhaps the stitching is tidier in the more expensive one, or perhaps there are more colour options or the design is more desirable. Sometimes, it will only be a matter of a well-known name, or a trendier, more luxurious branding, packaging and retail environment that makes the more expensive one 'seem' still to offer value at that price level.

People make decisions in an instant about what a product is like in terms of quality and value based on its price, and they don't usually even know their brains have been through this speedy process. If they know that ceramic teapots of a certain quality level are £75 in John Lewis and your hand-made one is £30, they might perceive it to be more 'home-made' than 'hand-made', even if this isn't the case. If they still like it, you may find them looking at it carefully trying to understand what is wrong with it and why it is so cheap and this can be confusing and will probably actually stop them buying it. This is because they will perceive John Lewis to have a good-quality product, but would also expect a well-made artisanal one to be priced perhaps even higher. But if your teapot is £120 but does not actually look as though it is better in quality or/and design as the one in John Lewis, they will also lose confidence in your brand and consider it overpriced. So in this case, even though your cost-based price might be telling you to charge £30, this is probably not the right price for you. In this example, perhaps you should be looking at somewhere between £55 and £100, depending on where you feel it can be positioned relative to other products.

Another thing to keep in mind is that just because a competitor's product is priced at a certain level, it doesn't always follow that a large number are actually selling at that price. That retailer or brand might occasionally have got their pricing wrong, or mainstream retailers sometimes purposely overprice something for a few months knowing that the item will just sit unsold in their stores during that time so that they can then legally slash the price with a red 'sale' tag on it and sell it discounted at a price they always knew they wanted to sell at. This is one of the reasons why it is a good idea to get to know sales staff in the relevant stores and ask them about which items actually sell more often and why they think this is.

The price of your creations affects your brand (i.e. how it affects people's perception of your company and products and the value that they represent). So as a creative, you should never consistently mark up using a certain formula and stick to it, no matter what. Sometimes, you need to take more or less of a margin on different products or at different times in order to position your price where you think it should be. For example, if you get a great bargain on your materials, and your brand isn't differentiated by being low in price, then you should probably still mark it up as though you had paid the usual higher price on those materials. If you don't, people might wonder what is 'wrong' with your work and be confused about this price and your brand.

I remember once many years ago, I had made about ten pairs of peridot earrings with gemstones that I had bought in Sri Lanka extremely cheaply – so I priced them at £55. They sat in my showroom for months. I couldn't understand why they weren't selling and wondered if perhaps it was because of the limey colour not being so popular. So then I reduced them in price to £35 and still no sales.

Eventually, I had a brainwave – I knew both £55 and £35 were really too cheap for the value of the materials, time and design, so I re-priced them at £95. They all sold out within the following couple of months. I'm not saying this kind of thing happens often, but it did teach me that customers won't buy at a price that doesn't make sense to them that they can't reconcile with the quality of everything else that you produce.

Case Study

Anna Scholz finds that price, quantity and quality are a constant juggling act for her plus-size fashion brand and recommends being able to work out your cost price to the penny.

When thinking about pricing, Anna advises that it is vital to consider where you want to position yourself. 'Price has been a sticking point with me and my business partner before; he tries to keep the margin good and very consistent in order to make sure we have enough profit margin, which definitely does work. I am always tempted to bring the price down and always wonder if this might mean that we sell twice the quantity. Actually, pricing needs to be all about where you want to place yourself. For example, you can sell one high-quality piece for £200 and make £100 profit, or you can sell ten lower-quality pieces for £20 each, and you still make the same profit overall.'

Anna finds that you have to make sure you do your cash-flow forecast carefully, and include thinking about how many items you can realistically sell. She recommends sticking to the margin and not selling too cheaply, as you can still have some higher-end ranges and some cheaper ranges across your whole season.

For fashion designers, Anna recommends getting the Zedonk app (now called F2iT) which is a piece of software that helps you to cost every garment down to the penny, even labels or swing tickets. It is very helpful to look at the costs of production really closely.

It's worth noting that it suits Anna's brand position better for her to sell one good-quality item at £200, rather than to make ten lower-quality £20 items and sell them for the same profit. Her brand demands the right level of positioning, and the price reflects that.

Case Study

Steve Shipman tries to keep his photography prices transparent and holds his nerve in hard times so that he does not compromise on his positioning.

Steve notices some pricing challenges at wedding fairs. He finds that a virtual price war can start if there are too many photographers at one event and warns against being drawn into this.

Steve advertises his prices clearly online and he finds that this works for him. It acts as a sort of filter for customers who might not be able to afford what he offers. He also feels that price transparency is really important for his market, and wouldn't want people to come to him and discover all sorts of hidden charges.

Like many who have run a business for a number of years, Steve has managed to weather it through some tough times. 'You have to hold your nerve when times are tough,' he says. 'The worst thing you can do is lower your prices. There is a perceived value in how much you charge. You need to pitch your price to be in a certain market position and, from your research, you know that price is going to be right for the kind of people you want to get coming to you. You need to stay confident that the right people will come to you at that price.'

Steve has seen people go out of business by trying to lower their prices too much in tough financial times. 'You have to redouble your efforts, get out there and network with venue staff. Drink lots of coffee and hold your nerve.'

Again, what Steve is addressing here is that he has to be confident in his price, not only because his work needs to pay him enough, but also to show the value of his work. He is being careful to price his work appropriately for his market position.

How to price something completely new

When starting a creative business, it may be that you are trailblazing or connecting previously separate concepts. Following the path that we are driven towards by our creative output sometimes means that our 'big idea' might come quite naturally to us. However, we then enter uncharted territory with no pricing model to copy. I found this with my own bespoke jewellery business twenty years ago.

So what do you do when you have no pricing model to follow? The answer is that you have to feel your way with a bit of gut instinct and ensure that you cover your costs, and don't sell too cheaply for your market position.

You may also need to be prepared to work for less when you are first starting out and are still learning yourself. In any creative field, the more experience you have, the more you can pre-empt errors and the more efficiently you can work. You also work faster over time. So creative experts with a lifetime of know-how and wisdom will produce something in an hour and to a higher quality than an apprentice could make in a whole day. You need to remember that you are working towards your definition of success and need to price appropriately for the first step along that path – not the last.

Case Study

Celia Persephone Gregory explains how to relate your expertise to your pricing while pioneering new creative territory.

When Celia and her then partner first started making mosaics, they got whatever they could and put all their energy into each piece using every commission as a learning experience. To Celia, this felt like investing in her education, because she hadn't been down the conventional university route. Sometimes, the client wanted something very specific and then they would charge more as this gave them less freedom. However, other clients wanted to give them a lot more scope and they saw those projects as great opportunities to express something of themselves, so they charged less because they were reaping different rewards. They also took on projects that they saw as potential portfolio pieces.

Celia feels that the idea that when you first start you are going to get paid for all of the hours you put in as an artist is unrealistic at first, especially if you are trailblazing in a new area where there are no others against whom you can position your price. She advises, 'You need to come back to what you are trying to achieve. The more experience you have, the more mistakes you have learned from, so at first your inexperience should be reflected in your pricing.'

Celia advises people starting out to be careful of accepting work on the promise that other work will follow. For example, clients might try to persuade you that if you do the first piece at half price, they will give you another larger full-price job afterwards. Celia says, 'Make your decisions based on the project in the moment. When people say this will lead to other work, that is nice but shouldn't be the leading factor in your decision-making. Agendas move on and people move on, so you can't be sure this will happen; that promise may not stand the test of time.'

When she started out, Celia learned that artists often get agents and considered this route but artists have to be willing for their agent to make a lot of money out of them while they might not make so much. 'A good agent wants to make money, so by understanding that and letting them make money off you, they can help you build your career and "value" in the world of art and agents.'

Value can be quite intangible and this is what the art world plays on as they create more value by building your career with you as a brand. She adds, 'They want you and your story while you as an artist build skill or concepts. Personally, I was – and still am – in a niche industry which doesn't quite fit into a standard art market.'

Case Study

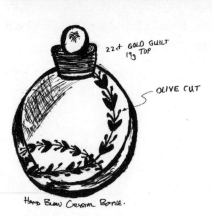

22ct GOLD GUILT 19g TOP

OLIVE CUT

HAND BLOW CRYSTAL BOTTLE.

Mohammed Jamal thinks it is vital for start-ups to reflect the value of their creativity in their pricing.

Mohammed has spent a lot of time in recent years thinking about how to price his perfumes and feels this is a very important area for start-ups to think through carefully.

'As a creative person, you are constantly measuring your self-worth against established products and brands, which can feel quite negative, but we all do it at some point.'

He thinks that rather than comparing yourself with a mass-produced benchmark, you need to look at what you are doing, how you value your skills and what you are creating and offering.

When he started his business, Mohammed began with a low price tag and he learned the hard way that the energy with which he learned his skills and the time taken to create the products is what really dictates his price. He says, 'I need to repay myself in order to be able to recuperate for this creative process. For example, if it takes me six months to make a fragrance, then I need to be able to charge for that and use some time enjoying myself by taking a little break, too, because if you enjoy yourself, you can create better.'

He feels that while you can work out a price by looking at the cost of raw materials and the value of your own time, it is actually value that is your ultimate asset. He says, 'All of us are unique in our skills; no two perfumers are the same and their creations will be very individual. So it is important that we value ourselves and our art and our skill and don't judge our offerings against mainstream products. Our offerings come from a completely different school of thought, where things must not be just about unit price and profit margin. We also have to include our craftsmanship. This is what adds the value.'

Mohammed advises that you need to believe in your skills and believe in yourself saying, 'It is like valuing a Picasso compared with a piece of reproduction art. When you choose a price, you are valuing a piece of art and the right price is actually whatever somebody will pay for it. You need to make sure you truly reflect the value of your craftsmanship.'

9

Money

If you are already selling some of your work while still in full-time employment, you can get a false indication of financial success. It may be that you can currently afford to sell your products at a price which wouldn't be sustainable if you had to pay your rent and bills out of that margin, too. It may also be that once you put your prices up to a realistic price point, your market won't want them any more.

So you need to do some proper financial planning. This isn't hard – there's no need to be scared. It is no more difficult than figuring out whether you can afford your household bills each month. There are loads of good books and one-day courses on this kind of stuff if you struggle with figures, but I promise it isn't that tricky. This chapter will help guide you through this process.

Financial planning

I first did this using a simple method shown in the following exercise, which is basically just writing a list of numbers and seeing how they look. This was the start of something called a basic 'cash-flow chart'.

Exercise 15

1. Start a new spreadsheet.

2. Choose the number of things you think you will realistically sell in a month, along with their prices, and multiply these together to write down the money that selling this amount will bring you as income. Write this down in the top row headed 'income', and show how many products this assumes you have sold.

3. Work out how much money you actually need as income to survive on each month. Consider your own costs realistically – for example, perhaps you could do without dining out twice a week and those daily lattes for a while! Include your personal rent, bills, tax, food and all other essential costs. Put this figure at the top marked 'Director's salary'.

4. Now draw out rows for each of your other main business expenses. Include things like business rent, bills, phones, website hosting, insurance, cost of advertising or attending selling events and any wages if you need other staff to help you. These kinds of costs are 'Fixed costs' because they don't change depending on how much or how little you sell, but remain the same even if you don't manage to sell anything.

5. Using the number of items you've estimated to have sold earlier in point 2, now write down the 'variable costs' to make that number of units. These 'variable costs' are things like materials where their cost will change depending on how much or how little you sell. For example, you need less fabric if you don't sell many items of clothing, and more if you sell lots. This will also include things like postage and packaging your products to your customers, too.

6. Have a 'total' number at the bottom showing the outcome of this chart. You do this by taking the 'income' figure and subtracting all of the other expenses, including your salary expense, from the income figure. If the resulting figure is negative, your costs are higher than your income, your business will make a loss and you won't be able to pay all of your expenses. If the figure is positive, you have predicted that your business will work and will make money.

7. This simple chart will show you roughly how much you need to sell to survive. From this, you can tweak the figures and work out what is right for you. Remember, if you go back and change the amount you sell, you must then go back and change the variable costs as well.

Example

My Initial Monthly Financial Chart

Income	
Standard bag sales @ £125 each – 12 per month	£1,500
Deluxe bag sales @ £300 each – 2 per month	£600
Small zip purse sales @ £15 each – 4 per month	£60
Fixed Costs	
Director's salary, which comprises:	
- My home rent	£550
- Home bills	£180
- My food	£120
- Home transport	£85
Phones including Internet	£65
Website hosting	£25
Business insurance	£80
Business rent (zero as from home for now)	£0
Business rates (zero as from home for now)	£0
Variable Costs	
Cost of raw materials for above products sold	£650
Packaging and labelling for above products sold	£25
Marketing – trade shows, events etc.	£80
Advertising costs – Facebook ads etc.	£40
Tax payments	£100
Shipping costs	£25
Income minus Fixed and Variable Costs	£135

You can use this chart to work out the minimum number of products you have to sell each month in order to break even, which is always a good figure to check that you don't dip below. You can also easily see how selling a few more products each month can make a massive difference to your 'bottom line'.

Once you are happy with your chart from this exercise, it is easy to extend the chart further so that you have different columns for each month. You can include a lot more detail as you learn and grow. You can show how those figures can increase when you get into more stores, for example. Then in a row at the top you can put in a figure showing how much money your business has in the bank to start with, and deduct/ add all your income and costs each month so that you can come up with your first full cash-flow chart.

Watching your cash flow

You need to find a way of working that enables you to afford to buy the materials for the next job; otherwise, you'll get into money trouble even if you are busy, because you won't be able to afford the materials you need to do the work at the time when you need to buy them in order to fulfil your orders. So find a payment system that doesn't leave you at risk from cash-flow problems. For example, if your customers don't pay you for six weeks but will order more in the meantime, how are you going to do this?

If you receive a big order from a retailer, it is important to get this in writing before you start work. Otherwise, you might invest hugely in materials, only to find that they have changed their mind. You might be able to talk them into giving you a deposit against the promised work, but this will be hard if you are a new business without a reputation to fall back on. If you do need a loan in order to finance buying the materials for such an order, your bank will be much more likely to fork out if they can see the official order from a legitimate business in black and white.

I thought hard about cash flow when I was starting my business. Each time a commission came in, I needed to go and buy materials, and expensive gemstones particularly, and would not be able to take them back if the customer changed their mind. So I decided to take 50 per cent of the estimate as a deposit at the start of the job and then the rest was payable at the end. This was still risky because 50 per cent wasn't always enough to pay for all of the materials, but it really reduced the risk and facilitated my cash flow. I still use this same system today and, if I hadn't, I don't think that my business would have succeeded. The deposit went towards the gemstones needed for each job and meant that I didn't have to find all of the money for the materials elsewhere.

Do you need investment?

When you have looked at your cash-flow chart from the above exercise, you may conclude that you can make the figures work but only if you have an initial investment. This might show you how much money you need up front to start your business successfully. Then you can decide whether this is an amount that you want to save up for (the best option if you can), or if you want to try to get a bank loan or other investment to start your business.

If you do need investment, you will need to have a very strong and clear business plan and financial plan to show your bank or investors. After you have finished all of the exercises in this book, you will be well on your way to having both of those.

However, many creative businesses start, as an alternative, quite slowly by, for example, working part-time while they start up. It is not true that you need a lot of money to start a creative business. I started my own business with just £400 – more than half of which I inadvertently wasted on some leaflets which were a total flop! However, a lot is going to depend on the level and scale of what you have in mind. Also, some types of business cost more to start than others. If you are turning your creative passion into a business, you probably have all the tools that you need already and might have the ability to start slowly and build things up gradually from there. So look carefully at your spreadsheet – you will find a way to make it work if you really want to. For example, perhaps you need to continue working part-time for a period while following your dream.

Miss Macaroon ♥

Rosie Ginday of Miss Macaroon started her creative social enterprise with just £500 that she had saved up and she found success through continually testing things. As you will see in the following 'Testing Your Market' chapter, this is a great way to grow safely, but not too slowly.

Rosie originally had a vision to start a community training and customer-facing space, but actually found that she needed to start a production-only facility for her macaroons first, with only an online presence, to build the business and make it financially stable. In this way, she was also able to test the social aims before adding the risk of an expensive customer-facing and retail business. The reason that she didn't start a customer-facing business first was that this was too financially risky and she found that she wanted her business to grow organically at first without investment, until she was sure it was ready to grow, which I feel was a very wise move.

Recently, Miss Macaroon took on investment for the first time in order to open a shop and Prosecco bar in the Great Western Arcade in Birmingham. The Black Country Reinvestment Society invested in the business and then the Big Venture Challenge matched this investment so it was effectively doubled.

It is a loan rather than an equity deal, but it was the right step to continue their business journey this way. Rosie says, 'I have realised my community and training vision, but via a route I was not expecting, so it took a bit longer than I imagined. I feel that it is fine for a vision to change and morph as you go on in business, and this keeps things fresh, too. You just have to keep testing until you are ready to grow.' She adds, 'Also, don't be too wedded to an idea, just keep testing and moulding it into better and better versions.'

Learn while you earn

Some people worry that if they don't work on their business full-time from the start, they won't get it off the ground. Often the opposite is true and they find they can start carefully without going through the risk of not being able to pay their rent while they build their start-up. Some people stay working at several different jobs either full- or part-time while starting a business; others find work that is very relevant to their business venture so that they can use this as part of their learning experience while they earn. For example, many creatives who want to sell in town-centre galleries find that taking on a sales job in such a place can be very helpful.

Case Study

Keith Brymer Jones took on odd jobs and teaching to earn a bit of money and to fund his start-up.

Keith began his life-long love of ceramics when he was just eleven. He decided against going to Harrow or Camberwell to study ceramics as he felt drawn to getting 'hands on' in a creative role, perhaps because of his dyslexia. He secured an apprenticeship at Harefield Pottery near Watford and enjoyed working there for seven or eight years. There weren't any other potteries nearby, so when the company relocated to Scotland, Keith decided to start his own business in north London.

He saved up and did odd jobs to find money to keep his business going. For example, he took on some courier driving helping a friend out. Then, he says, 'I worked out I needed £170 to keep the studio going each week. I devised a pottery course for a special-needs centre nearby and worked on that one day each week. This was personally very rewarding but also paid enough in that one day to keep me going for the rest of the week.'

Celia Persephone Gregory managed to juggle working at her full-time job alongside her mosaic making.

Celia didn't go down the conventional school and university route. 'I got involved in creativity when I was nineteen, but initially I travelled a rather erratic path. I think I'm dyslexic; even though this brings creative advantages, it can also lead to me jumping around and I sometimes think that linear thinking might be more helpful as a strategy to get from A to B!'

When Celia started working as a mosaic artist, she earned her living working in good London restaurants, which was a booming industry in the early 1990s. She enjoyed working in a different creative area with talented chefs and beautiful front-of-house presentation. 'There weren't many "creatives" around then in the way that there are now, and it was unusual to find somebody who was a self-starting creative. Thinking back, I can now see that it was right at the beginning of the era that we find ourselves at the moment; today, it is more accepted for creative people to do their own thing.'

At the time, loads of 'yuppies' were earning money through property, buying houses, renovating them and building restaurants, but not many were approaching this creatively. Celia and her boyfriend started to do mosaics and really enjoyed taking on all kinds of commissions in *restaurants and homes. As they were often installed in entertaining spaces, they were much admired, which led to more work.*

It was Celia's creativity that led them to pursue mosaic as a medium, and then the business grew because there was a gap in the market caused by the property and restaurant boom. Celia's restaurant work funded her start-up as she learned and perfected mosaic art. She found that the work went in waves; they would often receive a flurry of commissions and then it would go quiet for a while. Then Celia would get a waitressing job while she found more clients. She worked like this as she built up her experience and expertise.

As Celia got a bit older, she no longer wanted to work the long waitressing hours, so found additional funding by teaching. 'I did kids' workshops and adult education classes in mosaicing between commissions, which was a kind of evolution from the waitressing as time went on. It was enjoyable and paid the bills at quieter times.'

Case Study

Anna Scholz found that plus-size modelling not only earned good money, but also enabled her to learn a great deal about the fashion industry.

When Anna was thirteen, she was 6ft tall and a size 18. 'I couldn't find anything to wear and so it became a passion to dress myself.'

When Anna was eighteen, she was discovered as a plus-size model and she used the funds from the modelling work to pay for her studies, pursuing her love of fashion. She says, 'I was quite lucky because it was well paid, so only a few days of work each month would support me and leave lots of time for everything else.'

Anna moved to London in the early nineties and was modelling all of the plus-size ranges that were around at the time. When she started her business, she was still modelling for two or three days a month and

that allowed her to support herself while she built her start-up. Anna says,
'It was really perfect because I made a lot of contacts while I was working
as a model and learned so much. I saw the modelling as an opportunity
to really research the industry thoroughly. I found that the garments I was
modelling were all awful! The garments were really "mumsy", unsexy
and also apologetic. I thought that this was all wrong; curvy women are
beautiful and you should underline the curves and embrace it and go with
who you are!'

10

Testing Your Market

This chapter guides you through testing your market, which you need to do before you quit your day job, if you haven't already done so. You can easily do this in your free time.

Planning your test

What is the best way for you to test whether people want to buy your creations? You might decide to take some of your products to an exhibition, event or trade show. Perhaps you are going to try to sell them in a shop or on Etsy or just have a party and see if your friends and contacts want to buy some of them.

It is a good idea to try to stage some kind of event, because then you can actually look at people's body language and hear what they say about your work, which is really useful feedback whether it is positive or negative.

Don't forget to give everybody your contact details should they decide that they want to buy again in the future. Also try to find a way to capture their details if you can, like getting their email addresses. I found that a good way of doing this was to offer them a place in a prize draw for one of my pieces in exchange for their contact details written on a card.

Send customers who bought from you a brief email or card a few weeks later and ask them for any feedback. Really *listen* to that feedback and try to establish what is working, what could be improved and what your action plan should be as a result.

When I was thinking about starting a business, I tested the market while still working full-time. I advise all start-ups that if they are thinking of starting a business, they should make sure that they can run a small version of it in their spare time while also working hard in a full-time job. When you start up a full-time business properly, you will be working far longer hours than both of these jobs combined, so you will probably have to be able to cope with a significant amount of hard work to succeed.

In my spare time, I was making jewellery in my shed for myself and my friends. It was a passion with a view to something more. I'd be there at weekends and after work from 9.30pm, when I'd work for a couple of hours before bed. Many creatives feel this is like a hunger they *have* to satisfy and working late into the night is easy when you are feeding your passion.

I started taking on commissions for friends, then friends of friends. I made an opal sculptural ring for my friend Sarah when commissioned by her boyfriend. I made other pieces for work colleagues and their friends and I was even asked to make my cousin's engagement ring. Many of these people then started recommending me to their own friends and contacts.

About six months later, I had a waiting list of thirty-three people (none of whom I actually knew – they were all friends of friends). Finally, I thought I might actually be able to make this work as a business. I had done the best kind of market research possible by trying out offering my services. I had learned loads and was able to adjust my offering accordingly. I'd also built up a lovely portfolio of past commissions, all of which I had photographed carefully.

Case Study

Kelly Swallow tested the market for her patchwork chairs on eBay.

Kelly needed to generate some income for their family during the recession, so she decided to try to design, make and sell some pieces. She re-upholstered a couple of old chairs she had been given in her own distinctive style using beautiful, high-quality fabrics from an outdated upholstery samples book she had bought. She tried selling them on eBay in 2008–9 and ended up with a list of enquiries for bespoke patchwork chairs, so from this she could see that there was a clear market for her work. From there, she built up a list of enquirers and started the conversations that turned into a list of buyers.

Exercise 16

Write down what you have learned from your test run and feedback. Here are a few questions to ask yourself to start you off, but you will think of more:

1. What positive comments have you received about your work?

2. What negative comments have you received about your work?

3. How confident are you that the pricing is right for the market?

4. Are you right about the customer type who bought from you?

5. Are your customers pleased with the quality?

6. How many pieces did you sell and was there a pattern to the pieces that attracted the most interest?

7. Did others at an event you attended sell more or less than you, and why do you think this is?

8. How much money did you take and how does this balance against the time you spent making the items, setting up at the event and selling them?

When you have finished this exercise, have a good think about your answers. What do they tell you? Do you need to refine what you are offering and go around this test cycle again? What can be improved?

If your answers are not as you had hoped, you need to rethink your offering and try again. If your answers show you that you could improve something, then definitely take the time to adapt and try again. Your assumptions must always be re-tested. Perhaps your answers tell you that your product is right for a different market than anticipated and you need a rethink. Keep trying until you are getting orders and positive feedback. Only then should you be confident to take the next step and begin properly marketing your business.

11

Marketing Your Business

This chapter is about how to spread the word about your business offering and get the message out so that people come and buy from you. There are hundreds of different methods for doing this and you need to find the best ones for your own needs.

Telling your story

Press and customers alike love to hear stories of creative business people starting out. This is interesting copy for the magazine or blog editors and really appeals to customers, too.

As well as having your 'elevator pitch' ready, it is also a good idea to write down and practise a version of your business story that takes about five minutes to tell and another that takes about ten to fifteen minutes to tell. These will all come in useful when talking to customers, networking or talking to journalists. You can also then easily and quickly email these to journalists or editors who ask for them. Make sure that you keep it fairly succinct while also still including information that customers find interesting, like how you find your inspiration, how you learned your craft or what drives you to create.

Take time to tell your own story on your website or Facebook page, including plenty of photos and ideally videos of yourself at work.

Creative businesses are very lucky because, at the heart of each one, there is an interesting creative process and person – you! As you will have noticed, the public have a great appetite for learning about creatives and how we work. People often love actually watching us work, too. Have you noticed that if you are out and about at a festival or county fair and there is somebody glass-blowing, spinning or throwing pots, they have a huge crowd of people watching them? You only have to glance at Facebook or Instagram to see lots of people sharing pictures or films of people undertaking interesting projects with their hands. Whenever somebody is out and about demonstrating their craft, they will be surrounded by an audience watching with fascination.

Customers also particularly like hearing talks from creative people and hearing little extra nuggets of information, like how we were inspired to create a particular range and why we chose and sourced those exact materials. And, of course, those people are all potential customers. So this might be something you can use in your marketing. Be brave!

In order to market your business in the most effective manner, you often have to come away from the work occasionally and be a 'figurehead' for what you to. You have to dress up and stand in front of people and be interviewed and questioned and photographed even when you really don't feel like it. You also have to pick up the phone to people you don't know, be nice to them and try to convince them to run a story about your business. So be brave and remember that it is for the sake of your business and what you love doing!

Remember that how you come across will influence how people feel about your products or service, too. Just be yourself, and if that means coming across as a bit arty or disorganised, don't worry, the public will love it because they will sense that you are being your authentic creative self and telling your own story. If they enjoyed it, they will also share your story with their own friends and family afterwards, too.

Rosie Ginday finds that a combination of Google optimisation, public speaking and recommendation works for her hand-crafted macaroons business.

Miss Macaroon also supplies a lot of patisserie retailers, mainly in the form of white-label goods. When I asked how Rosie made this happen, she said, 'It is mainly about the Google rankings. But, actually, I don't tend to need to go out looking for customers as most clients find us.' This happens by a combination of Google optimisation and going to events.

I first met Rosie when she was speaking at a business event. She talked about the ways in which Miss Macaroon engages young staff and spoke with inspiring passion about her vision. She brought beautifully packaged macaroon samples for the conference delegates and, consequently, I know that when we open our next shop, I'll be calling them for our patisserie and I bet everybody in the room felt the same.

When Rosie speaks about her creative social enterprise, new clients follow. 'Take time to understand what's really important to you. Then you will talk passionately about your business because you believe in it and then you will find PR really easy because you will find that you want to get out there and talk about it.' This concurs with my advice about defining your business values at the start.

Rosie also reveals that when she got her first well-known client, PwC, this started a chain reaction and many more followed, and others from those. They have made macaroons for brands such as Ted Baker, Adidas, Orange, Pandora and Karl Lagerfeld and achieved this because clients recommend Miss Macaroon to others, and guests at the events also get in touch afterwards or ask for a card.

When you have a great product, a good niche and a good story with a social purpose, top-notch recommendations can generate a powerful marketing explosion.

Advertising

Advertisers will usually sell you expensive advertising space even if they don't think your advert is any good. They will try to convince you to book multiple issues or publishing cycles, and tell you that you can't possibly tell whether your advert is working without paying for several re-insertions – not true. I am afraid that they do not have your best interests at heart, but are just there to try to get your money, as most of them are not good at focusing on a longer-term prospect. Print advertising is really expensive and represents a route to spending a lot of money for little or no return. Even a small advert in a nice quality, local magazine can cost well over £500 and, even if your advert is lovely and professional, you are unlikely to get more than one or two calls from it because even really good adverts don't bring in many calls. Print advertising rarely pays for itself, and I have yet to hear from a creative start-up who found success this way.

Paying for online advertising like banner ads or pay-per-click on websites can be worthwhile as long as you think through thoroughly where to place them. This can be costly, too, so tread carefully. It is a specialist area for which you might need some guidance. Try starting with the free stuff like a Facebook page, Twitter profile, Instagram and Pinterest.

Press coverage

If you can manage to get a good story – or any story – into a newspaper/magazine/blog, then this will bring you more business than spending a lot of money on an advert, and is often free. For example, you probably have a nice glossy, local magazine aimed at your local area. If you pick up the phone, you might well find that they are interested in coming and doing an interview with you as local press are usually eager to feature fresh creatives. They will like to hear that you are an interesting new artist just emerging, and will want to take a photograph of you at work. This will help new customers find you and buy from you. In my experience, features always bring far more calls than adverts.

Some magazines will offer something called 'advertorial', which is where you pay a smaller amount than you would for an advert but the piece comes across more like an article. For example, it might be a half-page interview with you about your work with lots of photos, but you pay £250. Or you might offer them a competition prize in payment for a page article about you. This kind of thing can be worth doing, but you need to check you can definitely make it pay.

You should also try to get into national magazines or newspapers if you can, although this can be a challenge and takes confidence and contacts. Also this is often about managing to link a story about your business with something that is going on in the news. For example, if there has just been a story about how crafts are valuable for education, perhaps you can inspire them with a press release about how you teach crafts and that one of your students learned from you as a hobby while he studied to be a surgeon, finding that it helped him learn to sew neatly (remembering to mention at the right moment that you are starting a successful craft business). But do give it a go – occasionally, it works beautifully. If you manage to catch the right person at the right moment you can end up with a lovely national feature which could really begin to put you on the map. You can also talk about things like letting them exclusively see your brand-new range. In this way, you can make the most of the time when you have only just started and are the 'next big thing'. It is easier to get coverage when you are new than when you launch your second product range later on.

In my experience, emails to news desks and magazine editors who don't already know you are usually ignored. But be brave and pick up the phone or, better still, go there in person and wait outside with a coffee for them until they see you. It usually gives you a much better connection and will give you a much higher chance of achieving your goals.

Social media

I was chatting to somebody who runs a very successful and well-known yacht company recently who said that they don't do social networking because it is too 'low-brow' for their audience. So before you launch into starting a business Twitter account, do just have a think and make sure it is the right route for your customer types. Having said that, I think an Instagram or Pinterest account with occasional beautiful images of their yachts could be good for their brand, so they might be wrong!

For most creative businesses, social media can be a great free way to get the word out about your business. Yes, it takes a bit of time (more than you might imagine) but it is free. If your customers use those social networks, it can be a good way to get in front of them. It costs nothing to take a video of your work on your phone, post it to YouTube and then put a link to it on your (free) company Facebook page.

First, you need to make sure that you use networks that are the ones that your customers engage with, otherwise you'll be reaching out to the wrong audience. Some customer types might hate Facebook – my husband does! – while lots of people use it daily. However, those who don't like Facebook might love looking at images on Instagram or Pinterest instead.

Plan your posts carefully. Before you start, have a look at the posts of other creatives who you admire who have a good social media presence. You don't want to come across as too pushy or annoy your audience so much that they stop following your page. If you want to appeal to an audience who like creativity, then you should have lots of visual posts (i.e. more pictures, fewer words). Make sure that every picture you post is beautiful and 'says' the right kinds of things about you and your work that your potential customers want to see. For example, if your customers like the authenticity of you at your work, then show them photos of you in your overalls in the process of making your pieces, but if your audience want to think of you as a fashionable trend-setter, make sure you post appropriate images of yourself in suitable clothing.

Think about how often your market might want to see your posts. On Facebook, for example, it can be annoying if you see posts from a company page five times a day, but once every day or two might be about right. However, on social media channels like Twitter, Pinterest or Instagram, you can post much more frequently if you'd like to. One successful jeweller I know posts about once every three minutes and I honestly don't know how she ever gets any real work done, but she has loads of devoted followers as her customer type are never off their phones taking selfies either – so this seems to be right for her market.

Nanna Sandom of Splendid Stitches finds that directly approaching clients via social networking helps to market her business.

Nanna finds that Twitter and Instagram are her most effective marketing tools. Both are completely free. She uses Twitter to convey written advice and news to her followers and to engage with news stories, but she is particularly pleased with the clear business results that Instagram has given her and finds it easy and quick to take snaps of her work and instantly share them with her audience. For example, she might take a picture of a beautiful vintage dress rework that she is working on. As her medium is so visual, many of her customers are quite visual, too, and so often have active Instagram accounts.

She also seeks out vintage-interested companies and customers and follows them and often finds that this results in them following her back. She searches using relevant terms, looking through their posts and then she can simply let them look at her images so they can see the kinds of projects and renovations that she undertakes. Quite a few customers have come to her having found her on Instagram and this is growing, so she is really focusing this as her main social media channel now.

Case Study

Celia Hart uses a combination of social networks and her website to draw people to her work.

Celia finds that Twitter is a brilliant business tool. Like Nanna, she finds that what works for her is to follow people in a field where she is interested in doing some illustration and then hopes they will follow her back. When people see her work on Twitter, they regularly approach her for illustration projects and her products as a result. Her work often depicts gardens and rural life, so she seeks out people who are also interested or relevant to those themes.

A recent success story was when she followed a prominent garden journalist from one of the broadsheets, who then followed her back. Then Celia put her latest print on Twitter and the journalist retweeted it to many thousands of followers. Celia says, 'Over the following couple of hours, I watched loads of copies of this same print sell on my website as a direct result of this exposure. So it worked brilliantly, was easy and completely free.'

Celia also says that it is important for her to keep her website up to date, too, because people click from her Twitter account straight on to her web link. Twitter is all about driving traffic to her website and online shop, and so that can't be a letdown. She notices trends in the search terms that her customers use on Google (e.g. 'hare' and 'lino cuts' are favourites). Art buyers also use Instagram and Pinterest to search for illustrators who work in a particular style, so having her designs there has also been useful. Looking at this kind of information can help Celia fine-tune her website and make decisions about her product offerings.

Authenticity

Some designers and bloggers get thousands of followers on Instagram and Twitter and run workshops on how to gain followers and even take on other businesses to post for them. This does seem to work well for some, although I am not convinced as I think people can spot non-genuine posts and may un-follow. This kind of activity can leave some of the social networks feeling much more curated than they used to and can make the individuals seems less authentic. It will be interesting to see how that develops in the future.

Something I notice time and time again from start-ups is press releases or social network posts that look as though they have come from a big business. I suspect their owners think that this will make them seem more 'professional', but actually it will just turn off their customers who want to hear from them as an authentic creative. For example, I see social media posts from one-person companies saying, 'We are working on our marketing plan today . . .' Who is 'we' and why would anybody be interested in that? Much better to say something more like, 'I'm surrounded by paperwork today – can't wait to get back to my pottery wheel later!' with a snap of a pile of your papers. Same for your leaflets or websites; just be whoever you actually are and your customers will like it much more. You can still be classy and professional without trying to look like a bigger business than you are.

Another example is that many small craftspeople think they have to print out their price labels, while handwritten ones usually work much better as long as they are neat and classy. This depends on your market to some extent, but I can't think of an instance where your market would prefer your business to look like a bland and personality-free corporation. In fact, many corporations are currently spending big bucks employing digital marketing specialists to make them look like they have more of a personality anyway! So think of your authenticity as a gift, not something to hide.

If you can think yourself into the shoes of your potential customers, then it is easy to imagine what they'd like to hear or see from you. They usually want to see who you really are.

Celia Persephone Gregory finds that a combination of authentic visual marketing, writing and speaking work well when marketing her business.

Celia remembers the most useful piece of business advice she was given – it was by a friend when she was concentrating on getting her work ready for some big exhibitions. Her friend said, 'If you don't market it, people won't come.' This simple, great advice is very important! Celia says, 'You think you can just focus on making your work amazing but, sadly, that isn't enough if you want to make it financially viable. The making is only a small part of the business.'

Celia's career when she was a mosaic artist was pre-Internet and she muses, 'Marketing is very different in the modern world! For marketing our work now at The Marine Foundation, I find that I just keep doing all sorts of different things and the work comes to me from extraordinary places.' She recently won a big Mediterranean project as a result of giving a talk at a festival two years ago. Celia also writes a lot about marine conservation and has these articles released to the media. When people hear or read about work in this way, it helps build the creative's profile and sometimes more work follows.

When she started The Marine Foundation, Celia specifically wanted it to be highly visual so that it would work well on social media. 'My work is very photographically driven because people respond to pictures and I noticed that, on social media, people like sharing images and I like the idea that I release a picture and have no idea how far it goes. Sometimes, I find that an image of our work is on a front page somewhere through some really random route!'

There are amazing images of Celia and her team installing her sculptures all over the Internet. Once installed, many of the sculptures are designed with eco tourism in mind; for example, they inspire divers to visit and photograph them underwater, which, of course, leads to many more social network shares.

On marketing, Celia says, 'I could be more strategic about my marketing. The biggest problem with being a creative is that, when it gets to mundane aspects of marketing, it is really hard and a real numbers game.'

Awards

My business has been very lucky in winning a large number of awards; it's an impressive list we wouldn't be able to achieve if we weren't nominated for these things. The first time I really was just taking a punt at it, but we won and, as I explained in the business advice chapter, it brought us loads of PR and commissions. Have a go even if you really don't think you will win. I was really certain we wouldn't win . . . but I was wrong. For many awards, you can nominate yourselves or you can ask a friend, colleague or business adviser to nominate you.

You have a particularly good chance at winning any local 'new business' awards when your business is still in its first year or two, even if you don't feel that you have properly started yet – everybody who enters will feel like that, including the winner. I think that creative businesses stand out at these kinds of awards and seem more interesting to the judges than the endless stream of new accountancy firms, recruitment consultancies or the like. However, creative businesses rarely actually enter them.

Creating a simple marketing plan

One channel of marketing is rarely enough and you often have to pursue a range of activities. The way you approach the market is called a marketing plan. I know that term sounds a bit scary but, actually, this plan might be very simple at first. I'd recommend that you start with a simple list of what kind of press and marketing you hope to achieve within the next six months. Try to keep it realistic and achievable and make sure that every one of the points on your plan is quite specific with a clear date.

Here is an example of a very simple initial marketing plan for the first six months of a business:

- Create nice-looking Facebook page – put updates on there every day or two (usually images) and 2 videos per month by 1 March

- Try to build Facebook likes by at least 100 per month – first 100 by 1 April!

- Approach 6 galleries about stocking some products by mid-April

- Exhibit at 2 exhibitions or events each month – first one next week!

- Put out a regular press story every 2 months

- Do 4 talks a year to relevant audiences about my creative process, first one by May

As time goes on, you can enhance this marketing plan with more dates and by adding measurable outcomes and goals.

Advertising and the press was a sharp learning curve for me when I started my business. Back then, the Internet wasn't used much and things like blogs didn't exist. So if you wanted to reach customers, one of the only ways was via printed media.

I thought about what kinds of magazines my customers might read and gave one of them, *Vogue*, a call. I nearly dropped the phone with shock at the price of placing a little advert in that magazine. I think back then it was something like £20,000 for a page.

I learned that there is this thing called a 'rate card' which is a list of the different amounts you can spend to get your advert into different sections of their magazine. For example, the back cover is the most expensive and a tiny centimetre in the classifieds at the back is the cheapest. I discovered that nobody ever actually pays what is on the rate card; the prices are vastly over-inflated compared with what the advertisers actually expect to get for the space. However, even once you find out what you actually pay (about 20–40 per cent below the rate card) it is still really expensive.

Advertisers will always try to persuade you to book a series of adverts and will claim that if you just book a 'one-off' nobody will respond to it, claiming that if somebody sees your advert every month for, say, six issues, they might start calling. This is all nonsense, of course. In fact, trying to advertise in one of these magazines on a shoestring budget is futile.

If you can't afford to get really good professional-looking adverts, you could end up submitting something which looks a bit 'home-made'. You might well be proud of it and believe it looks almost professional, but it won't really compare to the other adverts alongside it. This sends out a silent message that your offering won't be as slick and professional, even if your work is actually far superior.

I tried placing advertisements over many years in various magazines. The most affordable option was putting something in the section towards the back of *Vogue* which is presented as a list of jewellers that the magazine recommends. It isn't a list of companies that they recommend at all, but merely a list of people who have decided to pay to be there. Back then it cost something like £300 to have a few sentences and a photograph in there, which was a lot of money, but it was considerably cheaper than any other type of advertising in *Vogue*. It made me feel proud to be in *Vogue*, and it looked quite professional. However, I must have had that ad in there for something like two years but only received about six calls from it in that time, only about two of which were converted into real commissions. The advertisers are really good at convincing you that you have to keep on spending the money every month. I'm good at negotiating, so I got their rates down, but still ended up making a slight loss on that whole advertising journey.

Now we advertise in a few carefully selected places (with much more professional adverts), but not because it pays off directly, but to keep our brand profile up. So my advice here is not to listen to the advertisers; they aren't really there to help you. They claim they are trying to support you so you can become a bigger business and a better customer, but they really don't know what you should be spending your money on.

Next I discovered PR. In my opinion, PR is great and worth much more than advertising. If you have a good story to tell or there's something relevant to the readers, and you even help an editor or blogger by writing it out well, they are quite likely to publish it. So write out your story succinctly and ideally link it to something else that is happening in the news if possible, and entitle it 'press release'. But when you are a start-up or unknown brand, you can't just rely on emailing out the press release as it will almost invariably end up ignored.

I used to look in the magazines at the list of staff, and instead of calling the editor, I'd call one of the features editors or an editing assistant. I found that if I could get them on my side, they'd convince their editor to run the story for me. It is also always better to call or speak to them face to face if you can.

I targeted a few specific bridal magazines, packed up a box full of my jewellery and went to their offices armed with a few names of the relevant staff. I'd just go to the office reception and ask if I could see them for five minutes. Somebody would always see me and I'd show them my jewellery. They liked my work and were pleased that it was new. I was happy to lend them some pieces for any shoots they were planning. Then I'd follow this by calling them every month and asking them what they needed for their next shoots. It worked every time! I think I stood out as an 'authentic creative' rather than just an agent. They would always be looking out for new things. So they'd say 'yes', they wanted something for a lilac bridal shoot and I'd send them a few relevant pieces. They would borrow them and send them back. However, they didn't always send them back without being chased and sometimes pieces came back damaged, so do be careful not to send anything too precious.

It wasn't long before they were calling me asking for pieces because I was efficient and always helped them out by sending the items clearly labelled, well packaged and promptly. It is all about thinking about how you can make their job easier and get yourself some press at the same time.

Another thing that sometimes worked was sending out 'press packs'. When I had a new collection of pieces, I would make some extra necklaces or earrings, box them up beautifully and send them as a gift to the editors, along with a press release. These went down well, although they didn't get me as much coverage as I'd hoped. I did have some success with it, though. I guess everybody likes a freebie!

When it comes to local newspapers, they do like an interesting start-up story, although it can be hard to find one. As a micro-business owner, I found that the best thing to do was to give them a call and be nice and charming and explain your angle. I used to try all sorts of things to get a 'bite' from the local papers; I knew that if I could get a story with a photo, this was all good publicity and I'd always get at least a couple of calls from new customers after such an article.

The very first time I managed this, it was with a very silly story. I called *The Comet* (my local paper) one day and told the news desk that I had a story about an interesting new local business (mine) and asked if they fancied doing an article about me. While I was talking, I happened to mention that I had two house rabbits running around my workshop (only because one nibbled my shoe when I was on the phone and I had to tell her to stop!). To my amazement, they said 'yes'! Hilariously, it was the rabbits that they wanted to feature alongside me and my work, and I never would have guessed that. I can still remember some of the dodgy puns in the article about 'carats' and 'carrots' – you can imagine! But they printed a nice little article with a big picture of me at my workbench with my two rabbits. This taught me that people really want to see your personality and your environment. It was well read and, amazingly, brought me six big commissions from brand-new customers as a direct result. It was much more cost-effective than advertising as it was completely free, and also presented me as a normal person rather than a faceless business woman and this worked well for my market at the time. Your local paper will often be very supportive to you as a new business person if you are nice to them and do what you can to make a story easy for them to feature.

The best press coverage was when we had something more significant to report. For example, when we started winning awards, the articles and coverage that followed this were extensive and valuable. We also found that once we were 'award winners', other press were always more willing to read our press releases and take what we had to say more seriously. Before too long, local and national press were calling me for opinions on bridal trends, ethical jewellery issues and entrepreneurism and putting my quotes into our articles without my needing to contact them at all.

Exercise 17

Research any local 'new business' awards and write down their entry dates and criteria here for any that might be suitable. Remember to look not only at general business awards but also ones which might be relevant to your particular industry. Schedule in at least half a day to write each entry.

Exercise 18

Write down the five national press coverage stories you'd most like to have. Then choose one of them and think about how you might work towards achieving it.

Exercise 19

Write down the five local press coverage stories you'd most like to have. Then choose one of them and make a plan of how to achieve it, setting yourself a date goal which isn't too far off.

Completing these exercises will have revealed some initial steps for marketing your business. The outcomes of these should be added to your simple marketing plan from earlier in this chapter. This mini-marketing plan will come in very useful in the next chapter as a key part of your business plan, and can be built upon over time as you develop your creative start-up.

12

Creating a Business Plan

When I started up, everybody I met seemed to want to look at my 'business plan', but even the phrase itself scared the hell out of me. I didn't even know what this was ... and it sounded really boring.

I was soon to discover that business plans aren't difficult or boring and can be extremely straightforward. They don't have to be formal, include business jargon or vast quantities of figures. A good start-up plan is often just a few sides of A4 describing your business now, your future vision and how it will work.

This chapter will go through exactly how to write your initial business plan and, if you have followed the exercises so far in this book, you have already written out much of what you will need. Start by typing the titles from the 'Headings' section below and begin adding a few sentences to each one which can mainly be copied out from your answers to the previous exercises in this book. You'll then easily have a whole business plan written out in no time.

How long should it be? For your first business plan, a good length to aim for at first is 5–20 sides of A4. The length of the plan will partly depend on who it is written for; if it is for banks or potential investors, it is best for it to be at the longer end of the scale.

Presentation

Type and lay out your business plan so that it is clear and professional, then you can easily tweak and change it as you go. You can also choose to illustrate it with some pictures of your work if you'd like to – there are no hard and fast rules. I think of a business plan as being a little bit like a CV, but for a business rather than for a person.

For a creative business, I like to see a little personality, whether that is within the type of language used, pictures or the presentation. However, don't get too carried away; it must contain all of the basic information. Keep it simple and concise, ensuring you choose a font, size and line spacing that makes it easy to read.

Headings

These can vary, but here are my suggestions:

1. *Summary*

Even though this should come first in the plan, it will be best to write this part last, so come back to this section once you are ready. This is often just a few paragraphs and definitely no more than two sides long. It should be an overview of everything that is about to be revealed in the plan but short and to the point, without much detail. You should start it with your 'elevator pitch' from Chapter 4. It should then include a couple of sentences, or a short paragraph on the following:

- What your business will be doing

- Why it is different from other businesses

- The history of you and your expertise in your creative field

- Whether you have already sold anything or got orders and, if so, how much and to whom

- A bit of information about staff, if relevant

- Information about location/facilities/tools, if relevant

- Why you think there is a market for your idea and how big you think that market could be

- Whether you need any funding and, if so, how much and for how long

People will read this summary before deciding whether to read further, so make sure it is well written, brief and interesting, but also leaves the reader hungry to find out more.

2. Current Status

Where are you now with your business? Are you right at the start of the journey or are you already up and running and fine-tuning everything? Have you been running a small version of your business in your spare time? How many customers or orders do you currently have in the pipeline?

3. Vision

This should include information about what you will be doing and why. Ideally, this should show how you align your creative vision with a commercial vision and some information on what success will look like to you.

You should use the information from the exercises in Chapter 3 here. You might want to include the visual version as well as the written one if you are proud of it, too. Say how your vision matches your planned company activities if this isn't obvious. For example, you might say that your vision is to bring Shakespeare to the world in a new way and that your hand-thrown mugs that have quotes on them will be your first product to fulfil this in a fun and commercial way.

You should say how ready you are to go. For example, do you already have premises, tools, customers and products designed, or are you still working this out? If so, how long will it take?

4. Values

Here you should show your business values from Chapter 3.

5. Product/Service

What will you be doing and how? What is your idea? What products and ranges have you already come up with and what still needs more work? If you have a great idea, what might you follow that with next? Briefly include how these products fulfil your vision.

6. Management and Team

This section should explain why you are qualified/able/talented enough to do what you are setting out to do. Remember that here you are advertising or selling yourself as the right person to run this business. If you learned your skills when you were eight years old, say so. If you have been working in a corporate world hiding a burning passion, say so. Also, list any work experience that you have and see how you can make it sound relevant.

If you plan to start with just you but have an idea of how you might grow things, explain this – e.g. 'I plan to start alone but within the first year I hope to take on an assistant/apprentice and also somebody to cover administration and bookkeeping...' Any details you have here are really helpful because they will show that you are thinking about future growth. It is great to include a preliminary time-plan showing how you think things might grow over the coming five years in terms of staff and skills, too. This shows you are thinking about growth seriously.

If you or your team need some training to help them, explain this and how you will handle it – e.g. 'After two years, I will buy an enamelling kiln and my staff will need training to use it, and then we will be able to offer a different, improved service.'

If you already have a team in mind, explain this – e.g. 'My cousin is a great administrator with a small baby and experience (details) looking for part-time work and I plan to employ her for two days a week in six months...'

If you envisage a large team, include a chart showing how the structure might work. And if you have a more formal Board in mind from the outset, then list who will be on it and why.

7. Market

Who will your customers be and why will they want your products? What research have you done to prove this? Use all of the information and explain the research that you did in Chapter 5. Show how you have considered all options and what your route to market will be from Chapter 6. This needs to be credible and realistic.

If you already have customers, explain who they are and how you will build that customer base, and perhaps attract others. What has been working for you?

If you have already tested your market in any way, show how well this has worked from Chapter 10 and how you have drawn conclusions and changed your offering to respond to this. Include your marketing plan from Chapter 11 as well.

Are there any market trends developing that you have spotted that are relevant? For example, Rosie from Miss Macaroon used the recent cupcake trend to predict successfully a macaroon trend. This helped the competition panel and, later, her Board/advisers to believe in her idea.

It often helps if you can show that you predict there is a much larger market based on the fact that you already have certain customers coming to you, giving some figures to back this up here if you can. For example, you may have a certain number of local customers and so can show that you can attract a similar number in broader areas as you expand. This is particularly important for any business and will be carefully scrutinised if you plan to try to get a loan from a bank or other funding.

8. Industry and Competition

Here you can show that you have carefully and thoroughly researched others doing something close to what you are doing. You need to explain why you conclude that there is a genuine gap in the market for what you plan to do.

You should include your research chart and SWOT chart from Chapter 7.

It is great if you can also include industry figures you have found online in any reports you have come across, perhaps indicating that a certain industry or sector is growing or backing up what you are saying about a gap in the market. For example, you might include information on a report explaining that millennials are particularly interested in individually created items. Trade magazines can often be a good place to start looking for this information but searching the Internet is great, too.

9. Operations

This means everything about how your business will actually run. Think through the following headings and write a couple of sentences on each one where they are relevant:

- **Premises** – here you should talk about any premises that you have or predict you will need, including details of rent and rates and approximate bills.

- **Supplies** – where will you get them from? How much will they cost? Have you negotiated good rates already?

- **Tools and Equipment** – do you already have everything that you need or do you need anything else and, if so, how much will it cost?

- **Delivery/Transport** – how will you get your supplies to your business and how will you deliver your products to your customers?

- **Security and Insurance** – how much is it likely to cost to insure your premises? If you plan to work from home, check your insurance policy carefully as sometimes it can invalidate your household policy. Is there any extra security that you need?

- **Legal** – do you plan to set up as a sole trader or a limited company? Do you need to be paying VAT? You can find out more about this on the government's website. Have you thought about whether you need your customers to sign legal contracts?

10. Finance and Funding

Here you should include your chart from Chapter 9 as well as information from Chapter 8 about pricing and any other details you can get together about how much you think you will sell, how much money this will make and how you will ensure you have enough cash to buy materials while working on other projects (cash flow).

If you are making any predictions or assumptions, explain your thinking.

If you already have or need any funding (including using your own money), you should list and explain this. If you are seeking funding, investors look favourably on those who have already invested some of their own savings.

Exercise 20

Follow the headings and suggestions above, spending a few hours writing your first business plan.

Reviewing

Once you have a basic business plan written out, you can enhance and expand it over time. There are many good books and online articles about business plans and you can make it more involved if you want or need to.

I would advise continually reviewing and changing it as you and your business grows and develops. Every time something important happens or you make a decision, remember to update your plan to reflect it so that it is always up to date, as if it was the CV of the business. Think of it as a working document which always offers a current snapshot of where you are.

It is a good idea to read and tweak your plan several times each year and then to give it a major re-think and overhaul every two to three years. As you learn, your plan will become more elaborate and you may also want to write out a separate marketing plan, team plan or financial plan.

13

Business Advice

This chapter talks about the benefits of good business advice and gives some tips and case studies to learn from. If you are a first-time start-up, you will benefit from some good-quality guidance. This can be from a local organisation that offers this free of charge, or from a family friend who knows the ropes. There is always somebody who can help.

A good place to start is the Internet. Search for organisations who give start-ups free advice in your area. The Prince's Trust provides advice and also significant funding if you are in the relevant age bracket. If you have a trade organisation, they might offer some kind of advice – for example, the National Association of Jewellers offer a mentoring scheme.

Here are my tips on finding the right business advice:

1. Trusting your gut instinct

If you meet somebody who is an expert on giving business advice, trust your gut. In my experience, if you feel good about them, then you are probably OK to trust them. Frances from Scabetti says, 'There really are some good people out there who do want to help a small business flourish, so you don't need to be cynical all of the time . . . just most of the time.' Conversely, if you don't feel a connection with somebody then perhaps this relationship isn't a good starting point for business advice.

2. Trusting yourself

Don't be talked into things for sensible-sounding reasons that don't feel right. In my experience, this particularly applies to people you might be working with and also to your friends. People will try to talk you into what they think you should be doing. Sometimes their ideas will be good, but they will rarely be fully thought through and might not be practical for your business; remember that you know your business better than anybody else.

3. Finding a mentor

If possible try to find a mentor who understands creative businesses rather than somebody from a completely different background. You might not succeed here, but I've noticed it works better if you find a like-minded expert to help talk through your ideas. I think that the ideal is somebody successful whom you respect from a different creative field to you, but who shares an understanding of your process.

4. Comparing opinions

If possible, find two or three different sources of business advice, such as mentors. Perhaps you might see each of them once every few months. This way, you get different opinions and advice and you will see useful common threads and learn from different experiences and perspectives.

5. Listening to your friends

If you ask your friends what they think of your business ideas, they will probably be unintentionally biased because they like you! They will usually say that they like your ideas, which might make you think you are on the right track when you aren't. So choose carefully – you want those who will really tell you the truth with no sugar coating. If you are lucky enough to have friends like that, brilliant, but most friends won't fall into this bracket.

6. Asking for advice

If you meet somebody you like and admire in business and they offer to help you, ask them if they might be able to have a coffee with you every now and then to help give you a little advice about your business.

This doesn't always work. One lady who I asked this of a year or two ago just politely declined, but she didn't mind and wasn't offended in any way (in fact, she said she was flattered). So what is the worst that can happen? They might say 'yes' and their help and experience could be inspiring and helpful.

I have recently asked two very well-known business people for a brief meeting to ask them about some specific issues and both happily accepted. It was great to meet them and their advice was really helpful.

Even when you have started to see some success, you still need guidance sometimes from somebody who isn't too involved. I met a lovely lady at a business event. She contacted me to let me know that she liked a speech I'd made and told me to ask if I ever wanted any help. When I noticed that she was the MD of a major fashion brand, I asked her if she wouldn't mind meeting me for coffee now and then. We now meet about four times a year and she is amazing and such an inspiration and a good friend, too. Her advice is always brilliant and sometimes we just talk things through and this gives me extra confidence.

7. Paying experts

Over the course of your business start-up and growth, you will often be approached by various experts who offer you their services as your business grows; they might be business growth consultants, graphics designers, marketing companies, website designers, accountants, advertisers, recruitment consultants – the list is endless. They are basically touting for your business and you can waste a lot of money this way. They don't know your business and you will often know better yourself.

To grow your start-up, I can tell you from many, many experiences that these experts don't usually know how to spend your business budget better than you do. I have often rejected their work and ended up doing the job myself but still had to pay for it.

Don't just assume they know better than you because they have a business offering that service to others and claim to be experts. This is especially true when you are trailblazing a new route in your area. There are a few consultancies which are good, but they are not common so please take the default as 'no' and only be convinced when you are really sure they are going to earn their keep.

Ask experts if they have worked with other small creative businesses, because many of them have only worked for other large companies where the client landscape and visual expectations are very different.

Also try to talk to the other businesses that they have worked with to check what they thought. I once paid a lot of money to a branding company who looked the part and talked the talk, but were absolutely lousy. I had been impressed by their list of other clients who always seemed to have good branding and strong adverts. When I spoke to one of those companies later, it turned out that they only worked with this company once on a tiny project and had not been very impressive. So all of the work that I had assumed was theirs . . . wasn't.

8. Respecting your mentor

If you know that you ultimately want to start a business, don't end up working for somebody else who is doing *exactly* what you think you might want to do. Yes, learn from them, take evening courses from them, volunteer for them to build up your skills openly, but don't actually work for them. I think that this can lead to you accepting their way of doing things as the 'norm' and stifling your ability to see the right gap for your own business. I also think this stifles full creativity. A carbon copy of somebody else's business is very unlikely to work for you.

Setting up in competition with them is also an unpleasant way to treat your previous mentor. I've met a few creatives who have fallen out with their ex-staff over this, and even met two where the situation resulted in a nasty legal battle as well.

A young lady who used to work in my company has started what seems to be a tiny version of my business, and so is not fresh or different in any way. This might work for a while as a micro-business, but won't ultimately provide her with what she really wants or do justice to her strong capabilities.

Case Study

Rosemary Goodenough finds value in both praise and constructive criticism.

When Rosemary had the idea of turning digital images into products, she applied to get into the School for Creative Startups, and was hugely disappointed to be turned down. However, with hindsight she believes it was the best thing that could have happened because it led her to re-think her ideas.

Rosemary had originally thought of putting her artwork on to many different objects, such as high-quality trays, placemats and bed linen. But the concept of a 'brand' had not yet occurred to her.

As Rosemary recalled in an earlier case study, when she overheard a lady at an exhibition commenting that she'd like to wear one of Rosemary's paintings as a scarf, she began to think of her business in an entirely different light. This might not have happened if she'd been accepted on that course!

Once Rosemary had produced her first scarf and designed her packaging, she gave one to her sister-in-law as a gift. Rosemary's brother, who is executive chairman of Design Bridges, was very impressed with both the beauty and the quality of the product and suggested that 'it should be the start of a luxury heritage brand'. This advice helped Rosemary to refine her offering and figure out the next step.

Rosemary has learned to value constructive feedback and comments from the community through trade shows, press, marketing and collaborations.

Miss Macaroon ♥

Rosie Ginday finds that her formal Board of non-executive directors provides extremely valuable advice and contacts.

Right from the start, Rosie decided to set up a formal Board for her company, as she wanted to apply for grants to test new training courses and to move to bigger premises. Most funders require applicants to have more than one (unrelated) Board member, so she appointed some non-executive directors. She discovered that the advice and contacts that her Board brought to her business have been key to Miss Macaroon's success. For example, one Board member provided a contact which helped secure Miss Macaroon's first major corporate order for PwC in London which, in turn, positively influenced other large, well-known clients. Getting hold of people willing to volunteer a little of their time to help you is wonderful if this works for your vision.

At the beginning of her business journey, Rosie entered a competition that unlocked a prize fund which involved pro-bono support from Shoosmiths, KPMG, PwC and Danks Cockburn. She received legal advice on trademarks, was granted an assigned business mentor and benefited from public relations advice. 'KPMG and Russ Cockburn from Cucumber PR showed me loads of support and their advice has been really helpful. Matthew Plant from PwC was my mentor and he was so impressed that he recommended me and I landed PwC as my first big client. Eventually, he came on to my Board, too. One of the best pieces of business advice I have been given was by Russ who said, 'No one will care about your social aim if your product isn't good. So focus on the product which has to be really good.'

Rosie's Board has given her great value. Perhaps the formality of having to report to it regularly has given her the discipline to stay on top of the numbers.

Rosie advises, 'Even if you don't have a Board, never be afraid to reach out to a few key people, especially when things feel really difficult. Generally, there are always people willing to help. Be open and honest about what you are struggling with, which will help you identify the real issues.'

As Rosie's business is a social enterprise, it attracts altruistic Board candidates. My own jewellery business is not a social enterprise, but I was still lucky enough to have a couple of years of great advice from a jewellery customer, Martha Birtles, who was a non-executive adviser to my business until she sadly passed away a few years ago. She approached me and volunteered because she really admired what I was doing by employing and training so many young, creative people and improving ethics in the jewellery industry. She had also recently retired and was very bored! She didn't want to be paid, but I enjoyed giving her regular jewellery gifts and a generous discount. There are many interesting and talented people like Martha who enjoy supporting small businesses and the arts.

In the early days of Harriet Kelsall Bespoke Jewellery, I was given various pieces of business advice. My husband's family friend, David Hawkins, was an older gentleman who had retired from a marketing role at Nestlé. I proudly showed him my first brochure full of made-to-measure chains with beadwork, which, of course, had been much admired by family and friends. The first thing he said was, 'This is not a brochure. It is a leaflet.' He also explained that the photography was not professional enough. He added that he just wasn't convinced of what I was offering as a business.

This kind of feedback was the last thing I expected and I found myself thinking, What does he know? He is from a different generation and doesn't understand. I was also shocked because he was telling me the truth.

We all went out for walk around his local town and he pointed out some of the jewellers. We walked past high-street stores and David explained that consumers put things in 'boxes' and see the shops as what they expect them to offer. He told me that it would be very hard to break into this kind of market. He did say that the customising angle of jewellery was really strong and that he hadn't seen anything like that anywhere, but said that he thought it wasn't enough on its own. He also knew that I was taking commissions from people and we discussed that, too. He said I should really focus on that because he didn't think it was available anywhere, but he couldn't see any reason for that. He felt that if I was really determined and could find a way, I might be able to continue what I had started with the commissions and properly break into that market.

When I got home that evening, it all started to sink in. In that couple of hours, I had learned more about the market than anything my previous few months of dodgy 'research' had taught me – mostly because I was only willing to accept what I wanted to hear! I realised that most of what he had said was right, but that nobody else had been brave enough to tell me that the 'brochure' and the idea of customised chains and beadwork just weren't good enough.

I was in floods of tears at the kitchen table that night realising that running a business was so much harder and more complicated than I'd thought. The breadth and depth of what I *didn't* know about marketing and customers suddenly became clear. I thought that maybe I needed to quit and get another job in London and just put my dream behind me.

As Tim and I talked it through further and went over everything until the small hours of the morning, I finally realised that although I had quite a few commissions flooding through to me every month, I had never actually *tried* to market that side of the business. I realised that the type of business I needed to grow was already staring me in the face and trying hard to market itself through word of mouth and my poor early website.

I knew that with my commission service I was offering something quite different from any other jeweller, but had always assumed that there was a reason that other jewellers didn't specialise in commissions that were properly designed for you and then made for you. In fact, it was really hard to get any jewellery made for you at all, let alone properly designed for you. There is a simple reason, actually – it is really hard to deliver such a varied service – but it was a reason that I was going to learn to overcome over the following few years.

Sadly, David Hawkins became ill and declined quickly, so I was never able to thank him properly for that couple of hours of valuable business advice.

Now that I had realised how little I knew about marketing, I began going to see two different business advisers to try to learn more about marketing and customers. I must have seen both a total of five or six times over that first year or two. One was Philip Gould who worked for Business Link, which helped start-ups with some advice; the other was Diane Butler from The Prince's Trust. Both offered free advice to start-ups.

When I first went to see Philip at Stevenage Business Link and explained what I had been doing over the first months of my business, we talked about how I felt that I needed to do more with the commissions and bridal side of my business. He was adamant that there definitely wasn't a market for bespoke bridal jewellery – something that I still like to tease him about! Like mine, his first reaction was that if it didn't exist in the market already, there must be a good reason. I managed to talk him round eventually, though, because I had evidence in the form of my ever-increasing commission work.

Philip also told me, a few months later, that I should enter the North Hertfordshire Business Awards. When he first suggested this, I thought he might have confused me with somebody else. I had been running my business for less than a year at the time and felt that I had made more mistakes than successes. However, when I thought about it, I had nothing to lose and quite a lot to gain from the publicity. I would never have had the confidence to enter had it not been for Philip urging me on. I wrote a very honest entry which was just two pages long which started, 'If only I had been right first time . . .' and proceeded to explain honestly about the numerous mistakes that I had made barking up the wrong tree for a few months before I realised what should have been my obvious business plan right in front of me in the form of all of the commission work that I had taken on.

I was amazed and thrilled when I was shortlisted and then won the 'New Business of the Year' Award. I ended up in all of the local papers and there were lots of pictures, too. People I didn't even know came up to me in the supermarket and said congratulations – it was like being a celebrity for a couple of weeks! Along with the publicity came work; at least eight people approached me after seeing my article asking me to make them bespoke jewellery.

I also found that people who I knew more distantly saw the articles and started to become advocates for me and these lovely people became a sort of 'network' for my business, which was brilliant. I had joined a local choir and several members began approaching me for commissions and telling their friends, too. The word was spreading.

I learned the value of awards and publicity and also the value of my own personal network through my friends. They may be friends predominantly but, if they like what you do, they sometimes also choose to be customers, too, or to recommend you. As long as you take good care of them, it won't damage your friendship to do business with them.

Diane Butler from The Prince's Trust was also a great help in our few sessions. I'd had to fight for that help because the charity mainly provides business funding to small businesses and then the advice goes with it to help ensure that the money has been spent wisely. I didn't need their money because I was just about doing OK, but I did want their great quality advice. I contacted them and explained this and, at first, they said no, it didn't work like that and they wouldn't be able to help. I wrote to them again and asked them to reconsider because I had been careful enough not to need their funds, but I didn't think this should mean that they shouldn't give me some advice. They agreed and introduced me to Diane, who was very helpful, especially with really practical insights, like how to work with printers and advertisers. She liked my ideas right from the start and was a great sounding board.

I really appreciated both Philip and Diane's advice and hope to continue to try to 'give back' to other people in a similar way by mentoring start-ups when I can.

Kelly Swallow found help and advice from friends and contacts when starting her patchwork chairs business.

Kelly's son had a good friend at school who visited for play dates. His dad, an experienced businessman, would often come to pick him up. He was interested in Kelly's work and would have a coffee and impart some brilliant advice which Kelly found very helpful. He also connected her with some key contacts, like the lady with an interest in mid-century furniture who ended up kindly coding Kelly's first website as a favour.

Kelly says, 'Business advisers can spring up in your life from all sorts of places and I have had all sorts of bits and pieces of help and advice along the way. I don't really think about it in advance, but often find that things come up in conversations with people that turn out to be really helpful.'

Exercise 21

Find out about anybody relevant who might be able to give you some advice. Think about friends, friends of friends and just local people whom you might be able to approach. Make a list of them and arrange a time to go and see them. Take your business plan from the previous chapter with you!

14

Persevering

You will come across all kinds of obstacles, especially in the first couple of years of setting up and running your creative business. When facing any one of them, it is easy to decide that you should pack it in and try something else. This chapter gives advice on sticking at it in the form of tips and case studies.

Sometimes, the only thing that separates successful entrepreneurs from those who fail is a determination always to get up and try again, continually learning from each mistake.

Here are my tips:

Positive confidence

I never consider that I can't do something – this concept just isn't in my mindset. I've had to overcome all sorts of obstacles; for example, I'm dyslexic and I had open heart surgery in 2013, but I still imagine that I can do *anything*. It is probably obvious that there isn't anything particularly special about me, so *you* can do anything.

Self-doubt will only hold you back, but inability won't, because you can do anything if you want to enough. Just take it one small step at a time and, if something just won't work out for you, maybe you just don't want it enough or perhaps you need to change the direction or approach. So to build your start-up, you need to work on both your creative and business confidence. You already know more about business than the person who hasn't considered starting a business yet!

A little fear every week is good

This is a tip that I learned from my dad; it is good to have a job that scares you at least once a week – then you know you are still learning and still alive. So embrace the fear – we all feel it!

The importance of being organised

It is crucial to be really organised when you are starting and running a business; and even more so as it grows. If you aren't a naturally organised person (or even if you are), get yourself some tools. There are loads of great apps now to help you with lists like the Google Calendar phone app and Evernote. I use my Outlook calendar not just for appointments, but for everything: to remind me to follow up on how somebody is getting on with a project, or even when to send a birthday card. Try out a few things and find out what works for you.

If you start in a disorganised way, you will quickly end up overwhelmed and in trouble for not paying invoices on time. This helps you keep a clear head and feel more in control.

Get an easy accounts app from the start

When you start a business, it is easy to feel bogged down with receipts, invoices, etc. Keep track of your incomings and outgoings with a simple app which will cost you next to nothing which keeps things digital by photographing receipts. At some point in your business growth, you are likely to need to move over to a proper accountancy system like SAGE. It is a good idea to have a quick word with an accountant about this when setting things up so that you make sure that you choose an app where the data can easily be transferred to SAGE or whatever your accountants want you to use in the longer term. This will save you a stressful headache later.

Don't spread yourself too thinly

When you start out, you will probably want to say 'yes' to any job that comes your way, unless you already have a clear picture of your brand early on, like Rosemary Goodenough, for example, who was determined to maintain the original focus on luxury. While it is generally a good idea to say 'yes' to most opportunities that come your way, do be a little bit careful.

It is often wise to specialise in what is working for you and this will help you focus your business activities and will also help you stay a little calmer.

I remember when I started out I was asked to do all sorts of things that didn't really fall within my specialist area of the design and making of bespoke fine jewellery – costume jewellery, tiaras, corporate gifts, communion silverware, napkin rings and even solid gold sex aids (yes, really . . . and more than once!). Each of these areas required different tools, suppliers or specialist knowledge and so were time-consuming. I did say 'yes' to most of them (although not the sex aids!) but, looking back, it did send me around in circles a bit.

Having said that, don't let this stop you taking on a project outside your specialist area if you really fancy it, but just make sure this is a conscious decision. I was asked to make a crozier (a big shepherd's crook) and pectoral cross for a bishop – for a small-scale jewellery worker this was way out of my comfort zone. I was really keen to do it, though, as he is such a nice man and it was such an interesting project. It turned out to be a great learning experience, where I ended up collaborating with a musical instrument maker and a snooker cue manufacturer, so it was brilliant! The bishop was so impressed that he talked about the project in his sermon and about how different professions and personalities can come together and create something beautiful together.

Coping with a changing social life

When you have to work all hours to start up your business, it can be hard to bring your friends along with you for a number of reasons. First, you don't have as much time as you used to have; also, you can occasionally feel as though you have developed different interests from your previous work colleagues. However, it is also important to remember that, at this time in your life, you really need your friends to support you and chat with you and keep you in the 'real world'. So remember to make an effort and keep up with them somehow.

For many it is a big struggle changing from somebody who had a thriving social life at work to somebody working on their own. Your work may be largely solitary at first. You can't easily any longer pop for a drink with work colleagues at the end of a day or just have those little chats over a coffee at lunchtime. And there aren't others around you to help keep you on task and motivated.

I found it really helpful to find some new friends with whom I had a business interest in common. In addition to this, I had to make myself clear goals around what I was going to achieve each day and then 'reward' myself with a couple of hours off and a trip to see my best friends at the weekend.

Case Study

K E I T H BRYMER JONES

Keith Brymer Jones has had to work hard and 'stick at it' through some tough times and offers his perspective on the benefits of resilience.

Keith's business as a sole trader went tremendously well and things were great for a few years. However, there have been two periods in particular during which Keith really had to mentally 'stick at it' and stay strong.

The first was when he had managed to land a great contract to design and make some beautiful minimalist vases for a famous boutique hotel. These were so successful that he kept being asked to make more and he was making good money. However, after doing these for a while, he began to feel like a robot making the same things over and over again at the cost of his creative satisfaction. 'It took a real effort of will to keep going and keep fresh to get through the quantity of work without feeling that my soul was being destroyed.' But he did stick at it and the work led to other more interesting commissions.

Another very hard time for him was during the late 1990s. A large, well-known national chain was expanding and really liked Keith's work. They agreed to order a whole new range of his items and he was very excited about the venture.

Once all the purchase orders were in place and he felt confident it would go ahead, Keith then invested in the materials and extra equipment that was needed for such a high volume. However, to Keith's horror, the whole project was suddenly pulled and the chain decided not to go ahead with their planned new stores. Now left with stock, equipment and materials but with no order to pay for it all, he was in financial trouble. And there was nothing he could do.

On top of all this and, in spite of seeking help from the Inland Revenue, Keith had to pay a large VAT bill and had no funds for it. So he had to remortgage his home in order to get the money together to pay the bill.

'At times like this, you almost have to become separate from the business and become like a machine and try not to get wrapped up in the emotional side of it. I had to be very regimented about going into work, throwing what pots I needed to and getting to the end of each day. I just had to take things one day at a time. It was a really hard period.'

But he did stick at it and, for those of you who have seen the BBC's The Great Pottery Throw Down, *he is now not only extremely successful, but a pottery celebrity to boot.*

Case Study

Anna Scholz has learned a lot through trial and error, and also advises that you need to make sure you keep your options open. She feels that doubt is every creative person's friend.

When Anna started out, she thought designing an amazing collection of plus-size clothing was really difficult, but now she sees that as the easy part, the hard part being to produce it all at the right price and quality. There are lots of tricky aspects, from sourcing to shipping. When it comes to manufacturing, Anna recommends a lot of trial and error. She advises that you test factories by sampling and comparing prices at different qualities, looking also at how quickly they respond.

'It is best to give them as clear instructions as possible. We have learned this from many mistakes. We got a whole run shipped and it arrived with every label sewn in upside down! It was far too expensive to send them back to China so we unpicked them all and re-sewed them ourselves, which took days. We realised they weren't used to seeing written English and hadn't known every label had to be a certain way up because we hadn't specified this, thinking it was obvious.' So Anna learned to give instructions for everything and pictures of exactly how she wants things to be finished and packaged.

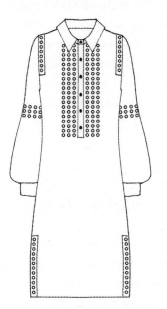

Finally, Anna advises that it is best to spread your manufacturing because then, if there is a problem with one factory, you still have others for back up. 'We have been through every kind of disaster, from cashmere goats freezing in the winter massively increasing the price of yarn, through to floods with our pieces being soaked and ruined in a factory.'

When Anna started her business, she regularly found herself on New Year's Eve wondering why she was working so hard. However, she now realises that this is part of a creative cycle. 'As soon as you finish one collection, you're bored and want something new. For the first ten years, every season two weeks before the trade shows, I would look at the collection and think that I was wrong about everything! But then, when it was all coming together a few days before the show, I realised I loved it again. Really, doubt is every creative person's friend because it pushes you to do better for the next season.'

There were also several times when I felt I had to grit my teeth and 'stick at it', too. One of the first of these was a severe financial challenge when we were very badly let down by some software engineers who were supposed to be coding a new website for us but turned out to be incompetent. But looking back over the years, the things I found even more challenging were much more personal.

When my team grew to about 20–25 staff members, it felt quite lonely at the top sometimes. When we were a really tiny team of less than ten, we were all friends as well as colleagues but, as things grew, this became more difficult somehow and this confused me and felt out of my control. I had previously always stayed a bit late and there had always been time for a chat and maybe some socialising after work.

However, after I'd had my two wonderful babies, I had to dash home at 6.00pm sharp instead to take over childcare and then I'd work more at home when my kids were in bed. This meant an end to casual, informal chats at the end of the day and popping for a drink without planning. As I left, I would notice how my team would socialise and invite each other to their parties or weddings. I loved seeing how well they all got on but, on a selfish note, I was almost never invited along. I knew that I shouldn't take this personally as I couldn't really come anyway, but I still found not even being invited really hard for a while.

I felt that I was trying my best under really difficult circumstances to do everything for my team members and to help their careers grow and flourish and to provide them with a positive environment. I was juggling motherhood and work which was so hard, trying to keep opportunities for their development coming their way. Despite this, I had a feeling that a few of them didn't think this was enough and always wanted more from me – more money, more promotions, more of my time.

It is strange being a female leader. If you behave in too typically 'feminine' a way, people don't respect you. If you act in a more typically 'masculine' way, people think you are cold, even though they would never think the same way of a man doing and saying exactly the same things. It is hard just to get on and do the job without being judged as a human being.

During this period, it took all my strength to keep going. I had also been struggling through some personal issues, including several miscarriages and then eight months of post-natal depression. As a person who is always wildly optimistic and positive, all this was hard for me to get through as I just wasn't emotionally equipped to deal with feeling dark and bleak. It was as though I'd had a personality transplant.

However, I did stick at it and, thanks to a brilliant husband, an amazing team and some wonderful friends, I soon arrived at much happier times. It is now hard for me to think myself into how I felt back then, as it seems like a distant memory.

Over the years, I have discovered that it is all right to let your human side show through every now and then and to be seen to be affected by a difficult emotional situation at work rather than hiding it. However, you also need to remain professional as well. It sounds cheesy, but you do just need to be yourself. But even knowing this, it is still a hard balance to get right.

15

Changing Direction

There are likely to be times over the course of your start-up when you find that you have made a larger mistake or perhaps when you need to rethink and change direction. This can be hard to do because your pride might prevent you from rethinking something that you have been so committed to for so long. This chapter gives you an alternative perspective, and guides you with some advice and case studies from those who have managed this change.

Here are my three tips on how to be brave and rethink if you need to:

1. Never be afraid to make mistakes

I've made loads of mistakes, but never failed to learn a lot from them. Without these mistakes, I don't think I could have found success. So don't be afraid of getting it wrong and trying again.

Case Study

Celia Persephone Gregory learned that mistakes can show you a new way forward.

It can be misleading to always feel that you must align perfection with success. Celia says, 'Mistakes can also open you up. You might get caught up in perfection. Years ago, I was taught this by a glass artist who explained to me that when something cracked, she didn't just throw it away but instead worked with that and developed the piece in a new direction. This completely blew my mind at the time and was really valuable advice.'

So scaling this concept up beyond each piece of work and expanding it to look at a whole business, mistakes can help you evolve your definition of success.

2. There is always more than one way

It is easy to feel deflated when what you are trying to do just won't work out. Remember, there is always more than one way to solve a problem. Sometimes, you need to take a break, talk it through with your friends or partner and try a completely different approach. Be a creative problem-solver, not just a creative expert in your usual field.

3. It is OK to decide not to start a business, too

Remember that not everybody is 'meant' to start a business. If it really doesn't feel right for you to start a business, don't. Many universities and colleges have aspects of their courses which can make a creative person feel that they will only have succeeded in life if they start their own business. I have spoken to countless young people who feel like they 'ought' to start a business but actually don't really want to, and this really troubles them. Entrepreneurship isn't the favoured path for everybody.

As I've explained, you really need to rely on a lot more than just your creativity and you have be very interested in commerciality and marketing to make your business succeed. If these subjects turn you off, either think about starting a partnership business with another person who fills in those gaps, or just don't start a business. You can build a great creative career working with or for somebody else without taking huge personal risks and it certainly doesn't mean you are any kind of a failure – far from it. Instead, it means that you are focusing on what you feel you will do best.

I had to do my own 'rethinking' at the very start of my business – and it wasn't easy at all. As I've already mentioned earlier in the section on the importance of robust market research, when I first set out, I thought that starting a business meant that I had to do something that would fit into existing shops. It became obvious that I should have just been confident with what was already working for me, confidently launching a business designing and making individual jewellery commissions for people.

I fell into what I now realise is a common trap; I had assumed that a start-up must always copy an existing business model. I now realise that it is actually much better to forge yourself a completely new pathway if you can. When I found that there was no other business already doing what I wanted to do, I thought that it must not be a viable business idea and naïvely dismissed it without further thought.

After completing my 'flawed' market research, I went to a business support place called Business Link in St Albans and picked up leaflets on how to register a business name and registered 'Chain Mail Jewellery'. I worked on a logo for my letterhead and business cards and began researching exactly what different types of chain I would sell as options.

I bought a book on how to run a simple, book-based accounts system for a small business and taught myself all about incomings, outgoings, overheads, tax and margins.

It was 1998, before digital photography had taken off, so I took lots of photographs of lengths of chain and semi-precious spheres on my SLR film camera. I found that if I laid them outside on fabric in the sunshine this gave the best light, but it was really hard to line them all up perfectly for the cover shot. I also didn't have any way of doing proper post-production on those images, so I had to rely on every image being as perfect as I could get it. I couldn't afford to produce the 20-page brochure that I had envisaged, so I had to make do with a single sheet of A4 colour-printed on both sides and folded concertina-style. I had a PC with Microsoft Office on it, and I managed to put it together and got 250 copies printed in full colour at the cost of about £120.

Next, I had made some flyers urging people to call for a free brochure. I took them to the local printer's to get photocopied, guillotined them up and leafleted over 400 local houses. I waited, but almost no phone calls came. I think I had three calls, one of which was an order form from a good friend of ours who lived down the road. I wondered what was wrong.

It finally came to me with the help of some good business advice, that my 'real' business was designing and making one-off pieces for people. I began to understand that, even though that model didn't exist already, I could actually create it. It is possible to blaze a trail and I did just that, and it was something that ultimately changed the jewellery industry, but I was not to know that just yet.

Case Study

Hazel Faithfull changed direction from ceramics to yoga – and sees it all as part of the same journey.

After ten years of running her successful creative business in London working on a steady stream of interesting commissions, Hazel found the ceramics market had really changed. The new concept of 'paint-your-own' ceramics shops and cafés had begun to grow, which knocked a chunk out of her market. She was just about managing to earn a reasonable income but gradually lost her steam with her business.

Hazel took a course in IT skills and decided to change her life. After a brief stint in an office job, she took a foundation course in yoga, which had always been another passion of hers. She originally took the course just for her own personal yoga development but gradually realised that this was something that she wanted to take more seriously. She worked hard and now runs a very successful yoga business in Oxford.

She says that it is great to combine her love of teaching and her passion for yoga and that she always uses her creative thinking in her business. Hazel says, 'When you have a creative skill, people like to define you by it and changing direction can be seen as "giving up". However, my journey has always led me forwards and I use everything I learned in my ceramics business now in my yoga business.'

Hazel also continues to decorate ceramics, making things like 'Om' mugs and taking on special commissions at local exhibitions. Her passion for ceramics is still a part of her life that she enjoys.

Hazel says that success to her is to find your work really rewarding. Of course, you need to pay your rent and support a comfortable lifestyle, but she also feels very rewarded when she gives people something that they really value. For her, ceramics originally fulfilled that need and now she finds her teaching just as rewarding, maybe more so. She loves the group energy of teaching classes and is excited to now be qualified to teach the same yoga foundation course to others that she found so inspiring ten years earlier.

Case study

In 2009, Celia Persephone Gregory had been working for many years as a mosaic artist when she changed direction and founded The Marine Foundation, an international eco-arts organisation with a new approach to marine conservation.

Celia describes mosaicing as very labour intensive and physical, requiring a lot of time on your hands and knees. 'Glass is a wonderful medium but quite harsh on your body.' Celia also felt a conflict between the people who could afford art and where the money was coming from.

Then, in 2008, the recession hit and she saw a huge dip in the demand for mosaic and so decided to use this as an opportunity to research alternatives and wondered how she could consolidate her love of the marine environment and her creativity. 'I began to notice that environmental messages are generally communicated in a very negative way, which isn't helping the cause. For example, whenever you hear about marine life being in danger, it is with an image of a turtle with a plastic bag in its mouth or something. Pictures of marine life in danger make people very sad.'

Then she discovered the scientific and technological advances being made in developing new reef systems. After a lot more research and environmental learning, she put all of this together to create bespoke underwater sculptures designed with creative and scientific innovation such that they sustain marine communities and ecosystems. The artworks encourage coral growth and are fish nurseries designed to replenish the seas and encourage eco-marine tourism.

Celia had already moved into public art with her mosaic work, so she knew about this area and realised that she had to get some pieces 'out there' to show what she could do. 'With the marine project, I did a lot of work for free when developing the concept. I didn't go down a big investment route. I put time in and made things happen myself. My vision has been to create a very positive environment within which to talk about these big issues. Rather than giving people a backdrop of an image of that turtle with a plastic bag in its mouth, now they have a beautiful mermaid covered with flourishing marine life. What we do is very real with an integrity and positivity that runs through the project.'

16

Dealing with Success

Success can be wonderful, but also overwhelming. When things start to go well, you are so busy that you often don't really have time to enjoy it. This chapter will give you a few tips to help you cope when things start to really take off.

Look after yourself

Sometimes, being a creative person surrounded in life by people who don't make things by hand can be confusing. Others might not understand your hunger and passion to make, build and create things and how you won't necessarily want to work conventional hours. This also means it can be particularly hard to get your work–life balance right because, when you love what you do, it is easy to overdo it. But also, don't listen to those voices in your life telling you to slow down too much; to grow your start-up, you do need to put in more time than the conventional 9.00–5.00 will allow.

It is essential to make time to exercise and eat healthily. When you work for yourself, you can't afford to be off sick or to let yourself go and not be inspiring to your customers or your team any more. When you are a visual person who needs to inspire others, I think it helps if you look healthy and well presented. It is important to fit in at least forty minutes of exercise three times each week. Even if you find it boring like me, and it seems like a waste of time, it certainly isn't because you gain energy that more than compensates for those hours spent exercising.

Stay grounded

If you have successfully started your business and things are going well after two or three years, remember that it isn't all about you. There is a lot of luck involved and, if you start thinking that your business achievements have all been won because you are brilliant, it will be the beginning of the end.

Remember you are only as good as the last thing that you and your team created, and also that you may only be riding the crest of a wave that could crash at any moment. Always look around the next corner and don't relax into thinking that you are a good business person just because you have had a bit of luck and worked hard.

Keep innovating

Think around the subject and keep injecting new ideas into what you do. Don't expect the same things that have worked in the past to keep on working indefinitely. If you want to grow, then stay just outside your comfort zone at all times by doing new things that support your core business offering.

While our main speciality is telling people's stories in the form of their bespoke jewellery, we do a lot of other things that support that. For example, we sell lovely dress jewellery, run kids' jewellery-making parties encouraging young creativity, run events and open days and have our goldsmiths working in a glass-walled room so that people can have a coffee in our jewellery coffee shop while watching them work. There are always new things to do to keep customers inspired and interested. All of these things work to support and enhance our business offering.

Dealing with expansion

After about a year or so in business, I was able to start looking into taking on a small business unit five minutes' walk from my home. I preferred being able to walk away from work in the evenings and separate my home from the stresses of everyday work.

If you want a bit more space but can't quite afford a unit on your own, you can consider sharing. Alternatively, there are many not-for-profit organisations who will give start-ups reduced rents. There is one of these in Hertfordshire and Bedfordshire called Wenta. There are many in London, including a great one especially for creative businesses called Cockpit Arts. These kinds of enterprises are excellent because not only do start-ups get a great deal, they also come into a learning environment with other businesses helping each other out. So have a look around and consider your options carefully before you sign a lease.

Taking on staff

If your business thrives and you are struggling to keep up with doing everything, you may well need to employ some casual, part-time or full-time help.

At first, outworkers can be helpful – they might ease the pressure for you by working on your behalf in their own homes or premises – and you may be able to find creative people who can do parts of what you do on a pay-per-job basis. Outworkers can be expensive, though, and are not always reliable, so choose carefully. You might ultimately prefer to have somebody in-house even if they can't be a full-time employee at first.

A good route that often works well for creatives is to take on an apprentice to help with the more routine elements of the work while they learn. I can highly recommend this route.

You will often need good operational people to help you fairly early on. So when you think about employing your first person, you might want to think about somebody who can support you (rather than another person like you) so that they can fill in the gaps where you lack skills; for example, somebody to help you with administration and bookkeeping.

As you'll see a little later in this chapter, for my business I decided to go with a kind of hybrid between operational help and apprenticeship. This worked brilliantly and Deborah still works with me now seventeen years on and is still wonderful; she works as our accounts manager and is also a skilled goldsmith.

Managing others

Managing creative people seems to be a huge challenge for people who aren't creative themselves or who haven't been brought up with creative people and/or worked in innovative or inspiring environments. So you have an advantage here. If you are creative, you will often naturally gain respect from your juniors and peers and that is the first step to being a good manager, because they already want to learn from you.

Often, creative people think that management is an entirely different skillset that they can't possibly relate to. However, when it comes to managing other creative people, you may well be a natural. There are some basic rules that are easy to pick up, and there are some really good books and courses to fill in any gaps.

However, if managing others really isn't for you but you need to expand, then you could either look to employ somebody who can take on that side of the business or consider a partnership.

Recruiting interns

Work experience, apprenticeships or internships all need to be a two-way street. When I had my first couple of work-experience students, I felt I had to teach them loads and actually they weren't at all helpful to the business in return. Even though they did contribute a bit, I spent more of my time helping them than they did helping the business. So the balance wasn't quite right.

You need to find a way in which you can help them and they also help you in return. You don't have to offer work-experience school volunteers loads of specific hands-on experience, as even just being in your environment and making the tea, answering the phone and dusting the displays properly will teach them a lot. These tasks can be helpful to you, too!

Always pay your interns who are not there as part of an education scheme and who are not true volunteers; it is illegal not to. Also, when you are paying them, you will feel more comfortable about expecting some real work out of them so that your investment pays off. You only need to give them a junior wage. If you can't pay your interns but somebody is keen to volunteer their time in return for being taught, remember to think of them as just a helper who is giving you some time and not as an apprentice or worker. Having a volunteer means that you can't specify their working hours or insist that they come on a certain day – it is up to them. A volunteer does not have to take responsibility for any part of your business process and shouldn't do 'real' helpful work or do jobs that they don't want to do.

Some employers (particularly in the fashion industry) abuse young people and expect them to do the dirty work without paying them at all, which I think is awful. My own natural instinct is too skewed the other way but, actually, the right answer is to strike a happy medium.

Stay in touch with the really good proactive interns, as you might be able to employ them permanently once they have completed their studies.

Taking responsibility

Right from the start, you should think about the effect you are having on your environment and your community. This might mean ensuring that your waste is recycled, that your fuel is as responsibly used as possible or that you check that your materials are ethically sourced. So if you are starting up now, do a bit of research and don't just go for the cheapest supplier price without thinking about this carefully. This will also help you build a really sustainable business.

Try to find a way to reuse waste if you can, because this is always better than recycling if possible. If we make a mistake and over-order something, we don't just bin the excess, we think about who might be able to reuse it. For example, there is a great business called Wot-Ever Scrapstore based in Welwyn, which is local to our main studio. They take business waste like boxes, stationery, fabric off-cuts and all sorts of things and use it for school or community projects. We often donate old furniture to charity or put things on Freecycle or local Facebook pages to ensure they don't go to waste. We even take our ribbon-end trimmings to a local nursery so that they can use them for sticking.

I was faced with taking more responsibility myself – acquiring premises and recruiting staff – as my business started to expand. In my first few months of business, I often met my customers at my kitchen table and we'd talk about design ideas. I had a fairly well-equipped workshop in my tiny spare room by this time and was ready to invest in some specialist tools so that I could work in platinum as well as gold and silver. I was regularly still taking trips to my dad's house to borrow his tools and also just so he could give me some emotional support and cups of tea while I made really scary and difficult pieces of jewellery – like a job for a Countess re-setting a diamond right next to her two perfectly matched huge, priceless emeralds! Emeralds are really brittle and if I'd made one tiny slip, they would have been irreparably damaged.

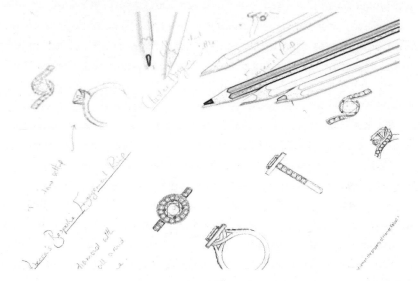

I began to use any left-over bits of scrap and materials to design and make a few pieces of ready-to-wear jewellery. I bought a cheap cabinet from Ikea and put it in my tiny kitchen in the corner near the door and filled it with my jewellery. Occasionally, visiting customers would buy these pieces but I found them even more useful as examples of the sort of things I could make to help people visualise what I was talking about or to learn what I was capable of making. I also found that if somebody was seeing me about an engagement ring or wedding ring, they often noticed the tiaras and other bridal jewellery in this cabinet and that helped them appreciate that I could offer a great deal more than they'd initially thought, and led to more commissions, too, without me ever needing to seem pushy.

I found working from home challenging because it was hard to stop working in the evenings when everything was all so tantalisingly near at hand. Also, customers were coming to see me more and more and it really didn't feel very professional seeing them in my kitchen.

So, after being in business for about a year or two, I found a tiny local workshop which was great value, but it was in a bit of a bad state and was rather dirty from the previous business tenants. I began to move in but, after having only got one desk through the door, I noticed that I had been bitten. I looked around and suddenly focused on loads of small insects jumping all over the carpet – it was alive with fleas! I called the landlord who quickly brought in pest control to fumigate the building – it turned out that they were dog and human fleas! Luckily, none had stayed with me in the hour I had spent there. After the fumigation, the landlords happily also suggested replacing the flooring and my little unit was clean, flea-free and ready for me with the bonus of lovely new carpets.

The village location worked well as it was very close to my home, was easy for my customers to find and wasn't far from local motorways and airports. I liked that customers didn't have to negotiate city-centre one-way systems and it was a lovely and scenic place to visit – more of an experience than you'd find in the standard retail environment. The only problem was that my Burmese cat always wanted to follow me to work. In the morning, she would meow loudly across the village green, pining for me. Goodness knows what the other villagers must have thought of all this, as she was extremely loud!

Having a place to do my business away from my home was great. I set up a little showroom, which I kitted out with Ikea cabinets. My husband and I held an opening party and Lady Verulam kindly cut the ribbon for us. I invited all of our customers and served champagne.

The phone just kept ringing and ringing and I was becoming really busy. Every Saturday, I would have about seven or eight hour-long consultations with customers about their commissions and then I usually had about the same number again spread throughout the week. I would spend the rest of my week doing everything to turn those projects into beautiful, one-off pieces of high-quality jewellery.

I would go to London once a week to collect materials, design and make all of the jewellery myself from start to finish, speak to customers wanting new projects, do all of my accounts, take photographs of everything I made (on an SLR film camera), scan and upload images to my website and try to market myself. It was hard fitting it all in. I worked extremely long hours (usually 8.00am–11.00pm) and often seven days a week, and I was hardly ever able to take any time off – even two or three hours was hard to find. Luckily, my husband was in the film industry and also worked similarly long hours. Also back then, I found I only needed and wanted about four hours' sleep each night.

I was working the equivalent hours of two full-time jobs. I also started to wonder if I could scale this up for a small team in the future. Even though I wasn't paying myself much (about £7,000 per year), the business was making a tiny profit, and I began to dream of a slightly larger business that I could clearly visualise: a small showroom and team of about five with different business roles.

One day I was contacted by a lady whose daughter, Mahailia, wanted to pursue a career in jewellery. I met her and we got on well, so I offered her a couple of weeks of work experience. This was quite challenging because she knew almost nothing about jewellery-making, but she was a very nice girl and I think she learned a lot. It was pleasing to see her skills progress. It also taught me that if I was to take on a junior again in the future, they had to be able help me out a little more as well as just take my time.

My cousin was looking for a few hours' work each week while her daughter was at nursery and so she worked with me for a few weeks which was helpful but not a long-term solution. Then, shortly after that, something stood out about a particular email from somebody called Deborah. She said that she worked for a large bank but really wanted to learn to make jewellery. She asked me if I could recommend a part-time course. She was polite and articulate and clearly computer literate (which wasn't that common back then) and lived about twenty miles away from the studio, so I asked her to pop over for a chat.

When I met Deborah, we got on straight away and I could see she was conscientious and good at her day job as well as passionate about learning to make jewellery. She made greetings cards as a hobby and she clearly had an eye for detail and dexterity. I asked her how she would feel about coming to help me by working on bookkeeping and answering the phone for the same kind of pay that she was on and, in return, I promised to teach her over time to make jewellery. Happily, she accepted without a moment's hesitation and a month later was starting work.

It was scary having to find a full-time salary. I felt a great weight of the responsibility as I knew that Deborah's ability to pay her own rent relied on my being able to bring in enough business to support her salary, too. I hadn't yet really paid myself other than essentials, so she would be earning more than me. But I had formulated a careful spreadsheet of costs, which showed that if she could free me up for at least a day a week within the first couple of months, I should be able to afford her salary on the extra jobs I could then take on with that additional time.

As it turned out, Deborah was absolutely amazing. On her very first day, she was already properly helpful and was saving me far more than just those few hours a week immediately. She was very proactive, a great learner at the bench and gradually improved over the coming months. Soon, we adapted her role so that she worked as the studio manager for some of her week and as a jewellery-maker for the rest, which suited us both perfectly. Seventeen years on, Deborah still works with me as our accounts manager and I often remind her that, if she wasn't so brilliant, this business would never have got off the ground. She remains not only the best employee that anybody could ever hope for, but also a great friend. So as you can imagine, having such a wonderful first experience of my first full-time employee gave me confidence to keep going.

As time went on, I also began to look for somebody to help me with the volume of jewellery-making. I had begun to separate the design skills from the making skills because, to me, they are very different areas.

I felt (and still feel) that good jewellery designers need to know how to make jewellery, understand a lot about what can be done with precious materials, comprehend a lot about relative durability and lifestyle and know a lot about what is possible. Then they need to combine this with impeccable communication skills and lots of creativity and a bit of innovation, in order to interpret a brief (and challenge it if necessary) and design the best possible solution. They need an element of salesmanship, too, in order to help the customer decide to go forward with the commission. While doing all of this, they also need to know how to pre-empt anything that may easily be misunderstood by a customer and to educate a customer properly about their choices and how to care for their piece. A good designer has studied design theory, process and history in great detail (usually via a degree route). However, while they can make jewellery, too, this is not usually their forte (even if they are good at it, they will be relatively slow makers compared to proper goldsmiths) and so the designer isn't necessarily the best person to actually make the piece of jewellery.

Conversely, I felt that the best makers are those who have studied making from an early age (usually via apprenticeships) and they enjoy the physical craftsmanship and making a piece to the best possible quality. But in my experience, makers do not often have the combination of design and marketing flair, as well as other essential skills, which are vital in capturing a customer's dreams and transforming them into their perfect design.

With all of this in mind, I started looking into finding external making talent on a job-by-job basis for various specialist commissions. I felt that I was pretty good at making and polishing jewellery, but my stone-setting skills were not so proficient. So for a while I had occasionally worked with a lovely stone-setter called Ivor for the trickier jobs. He had been recommended to me by my favourite gemstone dealer. And when I needed some hand-lettering done (which I could do, but not brilliantly), Ivor recommended an engraver called Mike. As I became busier and busier, I continued to find more contacts like this via word of mouth, like a chain of recommendation from people whose work I really respected. So I was beginning to get some very talented contacts for specialist parts of my making process.

Ivor's workshop was basic but functional and he was a highly organised, tidy and helpful person – I do miss him since his retirement. Mike's, however, was filthy! He would smoke while working and I don't think I ever saw him without a fag on the go. Consequently, there was a layer of grime and nicotine on everything in his dingy little room with no natural light. There was something about the combination of the grime and his workbench that made me feel as though I had stepped back into Dickensian London. But he was a great engraver and was always very kind, agreeing to prioritise our work above others when needed. He always did his best for Deborah and me and, if I warned him in advance, he would usually do a pile of engraving jobs for me while I criss-crossed London on my other errands, like buying bullion or dropping things off at the Assay Office for hallmarking. I often used to have to find him at the beginning of the day in the betting shop and prise him out of there in order to do some work, but he usually happily obliged.

I had also just begun using a small workshop in London run by a chap called Andy for a few of my simple jobs, back when more goldsmiths still hand-made jewellery in Hatton Garden. As Ivor said, they could do the basic stuff well, but wouldn't be able to handle any of my more ambitious commissions. They were five people squeezed into one room. They were very laddish and it was a bit scary going in there and speaking with them about individual projects. I soon got the hang of where to stand when talking to Andy so that I didn't have to face the explicit nude calendars on the wall.

At first, Andy and his team were a bit apprehensive about working with me and charged me some slightly over-inflated rates. But I talked it through with them and, once they realised that I actually knew how to make jewellery, they were much nicer to me and their rates came down. I think they had had bad experiences with retailers and people who didn't actually know about the craft trying to tell them how to do their jobs. Unless you know a lot about this yourself, your expectations are unlikely to be realistic. And perhaps they saw that I knew how long a job should take, so they couldn't get away with overcharging me!

Somehow, I earned my stripes and they ended up working with me at very good rates. However, they could only do relatively basic jobs so I was quite limited in the types of projects that I could give them. They also made a couple of mistakes that I had to pay for by not reading my instructions accurately as they were used only to very traditional and rather basic jewellery assembly.

I also gave a bit of work to a local chap who had previously owned a jeweller's in Welwyn but it hadn't worked out and he had been declared bankrupt. He had made mistakes in business and let people down, but he could still make basic jewellery. I thought he was a good friend and he did quite a lot of repairs and simple jobs for me over the next couple of years, then he tricked me into lending him some money to help him set up a new local business, which he never paid back. This was a blow for me, as I really couldn't afford to lose £1,200. I did learn a very important lesson, though: never to assume too much trust when working with friends . . . and always do the proper paperwork.

I also had an even more pressing problem than the missing money – I didn't have time to do all of my making and repairs and I had customers relying on their pieces being completed in time for their important deadlines, like weddings and birthdays. Ivor recommended a friend of his called Richard who he spoke of very highly as a talented and experienced mounter (goldsmith). When I spoke to Richard, we got on instantly, but it was really hard to persuade him to come to see me as he wasn't that local and doesn't like long drives. He was working for himself on a freelance basis but didn't quite have enough work. I'd asked him quite a few times and then, one day, he saw an article about my business in the *Daily Telegraph* and this persuaded him that he should come and meet me. When we met, we got on really well. He said he wished he'd travelled to meet me sooner and he agreed to work with me for three days a week, some days based from his home, others from our studio.

Working with such a talented goldsmith was a rare gift. Richard, like me, had a real love of his craft and it was a joy to work with him. He was quite a bit better than me at making jewellery and had a wealth of experience with repairs and advanced jobs. This meant that it was easy to hand over the tricky projects to him safe in the knowledge that he would make them better than I would have made them myself. But he could understand complicated projects and is very talented and experienced. He still works with us now all these years later as our full-time Chief Goldsmith.

I guess that I had also used much of what I had learned as a Computer Engineering Manager to help me recruit and employ the right people properly. This mixture of experience and luck was also critical in helping me find the other key people I employed early on and, over the next couple of years, I grew the business into a dream team of six plus a great Saturday helper.

The business model was set, the Internet was starting to take off and we had so much work we hardly knew what to do with ourselves. I needed to start to think about moving to bigger premises and taking on more staff, too. I had somehow negotiated my way through start-up territory and now needed to tackle the next stage of my journey by growing my successful creative start-up.

Contributor Biographies

Name: Dominic and Frances Bromley
Company Name: Scabetti Ltd
Website: www.scabetti.co.uk

Scabetti was established in 1999 by Dominic and Frances Bromley to produce beautifully considered, sometimes quirky but always desirable objects, made with pride and quality. Scabetti recently moved to two-storey studios in Dominic and Frances' home town of Leek in the Staffordshire Moorlands. Their base houses their growing team and provides the perfect setting for the development of their larger-scale installations. Passionate about supporting local business, they source quality materials and manufacture as locally as possible. By building and maintaining close working relationships with local suppliers, they ensure their clients receive a final product that surpasses expectations.

Known initially for their range of interior ceramics, Scabetti have built an international reputation specialising in the creation of bespoke sculpture, lighting and installation works. Both art and design, decorative and functional, contemporary and traditional, their work is not easily classified but viewed as an investment in every sense.

A mainstay of the Scabetti studio is their sculptural light collection titled Shoal, now in its tenth year since its inception. Fine bone china fish, each carrying delicate sculpted detail, envelop a light source creating a captivating sculptural form. Each fish form is prepared by hand as a fine bone china replica of the original design crafted in clay in 2007 by John Bromley, Dominic's late father and world-renowned master sculptor. All of the fish are made in the Staffordshire Potteries using time-honoured, hand-casting methods. Shoal743, a shoal with each of the 743 fish coated in 24ct gold, is now part of the art collection at the historical Fishmongers' Hall, London Bridge, home to one of the twelve great livery companies of the City of London.

Scabetti has also created shoal sculptures with steel fish, the most ambitious to date being Shoal No 8, at the Fisketorvet Mall in Copenhagen. At 12m tall, it comprises over 8,500 stainless-steel fish, swimming in a lemniscate (figure-of-eight) shaped path. Supported by an aluminium framework, the mammoth sculpture, weighing almost 1 tonne, was constructed in sections, shipped to Denmark and assembled by the Scabetti team within the shopping mall over a period of several weeks.

Shoal, Scabetti and the Scabetti roundel are registered trademarks of Scabetti Ltd.

Name: Hazel Faithfull
Company Name: Hazel Faithfull – Yoga; Hazel Faithfull Ceramics
Website: www.hazelfaithfull.co.uk

As a child, Hazel loved creating and this proved her strength through school. She qualified with a degree in 3D design from the Central School of Art in London, a great opportunity to experiment and learn the diverse possibilities that clay and glazing offers, including hand building, throwing and decorating.

An opportunity came with an enterprise training course to learn the business skills to support her craft ability. She chose to set up her own studio focusing on hand-painting English bone china using fine quality blanks from Stoke-on-Trent. She used her painting skills to work in vibrant colours which she then fired on to the china in a kiln, and she also occasionally created hand-made one-off pieces.

Hazel gained a place in the craft seedbed studios in Cockpit Arts and then moved into her own unit in Clerkenwell Green Association

Studios. She balanced the income of the ceramic studio with part-time teaching, educating adults in pottery and china painting at Kensington & Chelsea College, London.

As the business developed, she enjoyed painting commissions for life events and celebrations, working on everything from a huge plate to be smashed at a wedding to funeral urns for ashes. A useful sideline was colour-matching designs for advertising shots, and throwing soup bowls for supermarket brands. She worked on all kinds of commissions from hand-painted dinnerware with heraldic motifs, to decorative tiles for Mornington Crescent Tube station.

After ten years of running her craft business, the economic climate had changed and Hazel was ready for a shift in life. She now teaches yoga full time in the Hatha Yoga tradition with focus on breath and meditation. She trained fifteen years ago with the British Wheel of Yoga and enjoys a breadth of students with mixed abilities, ages and challenges. She feels it is an honour to watch people rediscover their optimum of wellbeing, connecting their body, breath and mind to find ease and calm.

Name: Rosie Ginday

Company Name: Miss Macaroon

Website: www.missmacaroon.co.uk

Rosie created Miss Macaroon in 2011 to combine her passion for social enterprise and premium-quality baking. Her ultimate aim is to help youngsters break into a highly competitive industry, while providing moments of sublime indulgence for Miss Macaroon's customers.

Rosie took an art degree foundation course and then trained as a high-end pastry chef at University College Birmingham, and moved on to working in a Michelin-starred kitchen.

Miss Macaroon provides fine, hand-crafted, gluten-free macaroons – whether they're to mark a special occasion such as a wedding, or to give as a gift to others. They can make bespoke logo-printed macaroons for businesses and designer brands for marketing and event purposes, and via wholesale to sell in their own establishments. As the only patisserie in the world that can Pantone colour-match their macaroons, they've had the opportunity to work with some of the biggest fashion brands, such as Karl Lagerfeld, Adidas and Ted Baker, and with other huge corporations such as Orange, ITV and Goldman Sachs.

Rosie is also proud to own Birmingham's first macaroon and Prosecco bar, which opened in October 2016, based in one of Birmingham's traditional Victorian-style arcades. They plan to open more bars across the UK over the next few years.

At Miss Macaroon, indulgence is also a virtue because their social enterprise activities are supported through every macaroon sold, helping to provide employment opportunities and training programmes for youngsters. The training scheme, MacsMAD ('Macaroons that Make a Difference'), is aimed at some of the most socially disadvantaged young people, like care-leavers, ex-offenders and those who have slipped through the education system. This adds an entirely new and unique flavour to the macaroons, and one that can truly be savoured and enjoyed beyond the mere eating of the macaroons – changing the world one macaroon at a time.

Rosie has received a number of awards for her entrepreneurship – winning the Enterprise Catalyst Social Entrepreneur award in 2015, the Asian Business Young Entrepreneur Midlands Award in 2016 and making it as a finalist in the Ernst & Young Entrepreneur of the Year Awards in 2016.

Name: Rosemary Goodenough
Company Name: Rosemary Goodenough
Website: www.rosemarygoodenough.co.uk

Rosemary Goodenough is a painter, sculptor, writer and designer who studied painting privately in Scotland and Italy and has exhibited at the Biennale in Florence and in many cities including Auckland, Barcelona, Berlin, Edinburgh, London, Milan and Salzburg. She lives and works in Norfolk, England, with her husband Michael Waller-Bridge, a portrait and abstract photographer. They collaborate in their studios, utilising their various skills and expertise, as well as working on their individual creative projects.

Rosemary's work is semi-figurative and, interestingly, she does not use brushes but instead paints with knives, cloths and her hands-on panel or board. The elegantly presented 'Rosemary Goodenough' heritage brand includes luxury fashion and lifestyle accessories for men and women, creating products carrying colour variations of compositions made by the artist herself derived from her own paintings. The brand epitomises the quirky and eclectic look of 21st-century English aristocratic style and was started following a remark she overheard at an exhibition of her paintings and sculptures to the effect that 'If that painting was a scarf, I would wear it!' Rosemary's creative trajectory into the world of fashion began with early collections that were taken up by Fortnum & Mason and Wolf & Badger.

Rosemary continues to collaborate with new fashion labels and designers like Consistence London and the tailor, Kimberley Megan, who both use her unique fabrics. Rosemary is currently very focused on building the brand in Japan, China, Hong Kong, Macau and Taiwan, as well as launching further products under licence following the success of the 2017 Rosemary Goodenough 'Hot City Collection' designs for the London Sock Company.

Rosemary Goodenough has also recently written a series of stories for very young children inspired by her drawings.

Name	Celia Persephone Gregory
Company Name(s):	Celia Persephone Gregory; The Marine Foundation
Website(s):	www.celiapersephonegregory.com; www.themarinefoundation.org

Celia's career has evolved over the years and has included over twenty years of practical creative experience. She has worked as a specialist mosaic artist and has been engaged on large-scale, exterior and interior commissions for public art awards, developers and architects. She has worked for the BBC and co-authored the book *The Art of Mosaic*. Celia continues to develop her unique artistic skill through private and public commissions, exhibitions and in association with galleries, and has now blossomed as an eco-artist.

In 2009, Celia established The Marine Foundation, an eco-art organisation which pioneered the Living Sculptures in the Sea programme. She works with NGOs, scientists and local communities around the world, making underwater artworks which are powerful interactive experiences that restore coral reefs and support the local communities who depend on them.

Celia has become an innovator with this creative approach to tackling the issues of marine conservation from a positive and fun perspective, inspiring and facilitating action and raising awareness of the issues facing the marine ecosystems. The photography of the underwater sculptures is very powerful and provides wonderful visual material for magazines and social media, encouraging sharing through Facebook and Instagram.

Celia regularly gives public talks, such as her presentation at Obonjan Island in 2017, a unique eco island festival destination involving the installation of an underwater sculpture in 2018. The Marine Foundation currently has projects in development in Malta, Mexico, Belize and the Bahamas. She has recently relocated to Aspen, USA, where she has been busy launching her new eco-art project #welovepollinators, a living land sculpture designed to attract pollinators. She is also working with the European Consortium on an Ocean Literacy Initiative.

Name: Celia Hart
Company Name: Celia Hart – Illustrator and Print Maker
Website: www.celiahart.co.uk

Celia Hart lives and works in a small village in Suffolk creating designs inspired by her enthusiasm for the countryside of East Anglia, wildflowers, birds, animals and history. She hand prints her work using traditional block carving and hand-burnishing techniques (she uses a wooden spoon as her press) inspired by Japanese and Chinese printmakers and the English illustrative print tradition.

Celia's father was a construction joiner and craftsman in wood, so working with chisels is in her genes. She makes a limited number of each print (10–50) and because of subtle variations, each print is unique.

After the Art Foundation Course at Cambridge Art School, Celia gained a degree in visual communication at Brighton College of Art and Design and started her career in publishing as a designer and art buyer for a major UK publisher. She learned 'the trade' by commissioning experienced children's book illustrators and designing page-by-page layouts with sticky tape and scissors. When desk-top publishing was invented, she designed some of the first books created that way in the UK. After redundancy in 1991, she set up her own studio and, for the next ten years, supplied clear, informative, digital artwork for major educational publishing projects.

Since 2001, Celia has concentrated on developing her personal brand of illustration, combining her love of traditional printmaking techniques with her digital knowledge. She designs and produces greetings cards based on her popular linocut and woodcut prints. She also enjoys working with designers and publishers on diverse projects, ranging from wine labels to decorative designs for music festivals, book jackets and café branding.

From April 2015 to December 2017, Celia was a regular contributor to *Gardens Illustrated* magazine, illustrating Frank Ronan's monthly column with a linocut, a 'dream gig' for her that combined her plant knowledge with the constraints of an illustrative, one-colour print. In June 2015, she redesigned the *Telegraph* newspaper crest for the 160th anniversary of the new-look daily paper, taking delight in re-instigating the telegraph poles and wires and introducing some jauntiness to the national flower emblems.

Name: Mohammed Jamal
Company Name: Jamal Perfumers London
Website: www.jamalperfumers.com

British master perfumer and cosmetic chemist Mohammed Jamal has over twenty-five years' experience in the perfume and cosmetics industry. His introduction to the world of scent began as an inquisitive six-year-old, helping out in his family attar perfume business. This early interest led to him reading cosmetic science at university and a subsequent professional career, which included working for global creative fragrance houses Symrise GmbH and CPL Aromas in the UK and Paris.

Mohammed draws on all the elements of his cultural heritage when creating scents for clients. Born in Malawi, he emigrated with his family to Leicester in the UK before settling permanently in London. He is proud of his combined British, Indian, African, Arabic and Muslim identity, and relishes the role that London plays in the modern world – freely accepting new influences, yet at the same time cherishing its history. His scents combine the traditions of eastern perfumery with a brand heritage that is proudly British and specifically London.

He studied entrepreneurship at the University of Cambridge Judge Business School, where his focus of study was developing a perfumery business model for creating bespoke scents that enhance people's mental and emotional wellbeing; for example, helping to reduce anxiety, depression and stress. He then relaunched Jamal Perfumers London in winter 2017 with the introduction of its bespoke perfumery service and fragrance events in the UK and internationally.

Mohammed's business model involves the acquisition of primary olfactive data (through interactions with clients) which can be used to understand how different plants contribute to healthy human environments.

He is a Fellow of the Royal Society of Arts, and a member of the Society of Cosmetic Scientists and the British Society of Perfumers.

Name:	Keith Brymer Jones
Company Name(s):	Keith Brymer Jones; MAKE International
Website(s):	www.keithbrymerjones.com;
	www.makeinternational.com

Keith Brymer Jones is a British designer who has been using traditional craft methods to make modern ceramics for over three decades. Keith's design philosophy is a simple one: to create stylish yet simple products that are pleasing to the eye, practical in the modern home and make people happy. The 'Word' range embodies Keith's signature style – exceptional ceramics that are durable enough for everyday use.

Keith has been involved with clay all his adult life. At eighteen years old, he started as a clay boy while doing his apprenticeship at Harefield Pottery. His tasks were sweeping the floor, making the clay body used in the pottery, and preparing the clay, predominantly for throwing. He later became one of their master throwers. In 1989, the owners of Harefield Pottery relocated to Inverness. At the time, Keith was the lead singer in a band playing the London gig circuit so declined the move to Scotland, preferring to stay in London. So he started his own pottery studio in Highgate.

His first commission was hand-making a range for Heal's in Tottenham Court Road and he went on to design and hand-make ceramic ranges for Habitat, Conran and Laura Ashley and then later for Marks and Spencer, Ted Baker, Monsoon, Bergdorf Goodman, Barneys New York and Anthropology.

In 2008, Keith met entrepreneur Dominic Speelman who asked Keith to join his company, MAKE International. Together, the two have expanded the internationally successful Keith Brymer Jones brand. Their company also takes on other brands, designing and encouraging the growth of MAKE's brand portfolio.

When Keith was asked to be a judge on *The Great British Pottery Throw Down*, he considered it a great honour to help the show have an enormous positive impact on ceramics in Britain. He feels privileged to help expose the wonderful experience of working with clay, both creatively and spiritually.

Name: Nanna Sandom
Company Name: Splendid Stitches
Website: www.splendidstitches.co.uk

Splendid Stitches' mission is to get beautiful vintage garments worn and loved by their current owners by ensuring the pieces are expertly altered and repaired.

The specialist vintage clothes alterations and repair service was thought up by Nanna Sandom on a cold February evening in 2010 after another large shipment of second-hand clothes from eBay landed on her doormat. Having always made and altered her own clothes, she started tentatively asking friends and family if they needed any clothes altered or repaired, and word spread like wildfire. After three months, Nanna decided to decrease her hours working for a large publishing house to dedicate one day per week to the new enterprise, while raising a young family.

Splendid Stitches has been a full-time business since 2015 when it outgrew the spare bedroom. It is now located in a beautiful studio in Bloomsbury, central London, and customers range from the dedicated clothes collector to brides-to-be getting married in their grandmother's wedding dress.

Taking pride in high levels of craftsmanship, attention to detail and treating each customer and piece of clothing with individual care, Splendid Stitches' services include everything from standard repairs to relining, reshaping and remodelling. They rework vintage wedding dresses and make garments based on a loved but worn-out vintage piece.

With a strong ethical influence, Splendid Stitches has been advocating 'vintage' as a conscious consumer choice from the outset; every vintage garment bought and worn is one less garment ending up in landfill and one less new piece made from scratch, with all the environmental issues that brings with it. Splendid Stitches is also a body-positive organisation with the fundamental line that you need to get your clothes to fit you, not you to fit the clothes.

Name:	Anna Scholz
Company Name:	Anna Scholz Ltd
Website:	www.annascholz.com

Anna grew up in Germany surrounded by good design, whether it was her dad's influence from running a successful advertising agency or her mum's beautiful wardrobe. At thirteen in the 1980s, she was 6ft tall and a size 16, and it wasn't easy to find stylish, young clothes. She decided there and then to make clothes that would make her feel and look great and started sewing, determined to change the plus-size industry.

In her teens she started working as a plus-size model, continuing to experience a complete lack of well-designed, sexy, plus-size clothing, so she saw a huge opportunity in the market. While studying fashion design at Central St Martin's College of Art and Design in London, she opened a small shop in Portobello Market with a couple of friends and started selling her own designs.

Anna's big break came when American retail giant, Lane Bryant, ordered from her first collection, selling it in their top-ten stores as a premium brand. The collaboration enabled Anna to move her design studio out of her home and into Ladbroke Grove... and so the annascholz label was born.

Anna has always believed that you shouldn't hide behind clothes; you should feel proud of your body and accentuate your curves rather than cover them up. Her designs are about femininity, glamour and confidence, offering the luxury and originality of a designer brand to the plus-size customer.

Over the years, Anna has designed diffusion collections for Debenhams, Simply Be and currently works with the German company Sheego. She has been stocked in some of the best stores around the world from Bloomingdale's, Saks and Neiman Marcus to Harrods and Selfridges. Celebrities wearing annascholz include Adele, Ashley Graham, Aretha Franklin, Dawn French, Queen Latifah, Lisa Riley and Brooke Hogan. TV appearances include *Mary Queen of Shops* with Mary Portas, *NDR Talk Show*, *Trinny & Susannah* and *The Fashion Hero*.

In 2016, after listening to customers, she made the decision to sell the annascholz collection exclusively online and stop stocking retailers so that she can offer better priced designs more frequently with eight mini-collections a year.

Anna won the Best Plus-Size Designer at the British Plus-Size Awards in 2015.

Name: Steve Shipman
Company Name: Steve Shipman Photography
Website: www.steveshipmanphotography.com

Steve is a full-time professional photographer who started his career photographing people for magazines, and built a reputation for beautiful and consistently well-executed photography. He worked for magazines including the *Sunday Times, You, Radio Times, Cosmopolitan, Marie Claire, Top Gear* and many more quality publications. He is very proud to have several of his celebrity classics included in the National Portrait Gallery's permanent collection in London.

About fifteen years ago, Steve photographed a friend's wedding for the first time on a new digital camera. It was a revelation. With documentary wedding photography, incorporating eye-catching, contemporary portraits, he realised that he could record a wedding day in a fun and lively way, discreet but creative, with a nod to his magazine work, and with images composed for the pages of beautiful wedding albums. He never looked back, and now thoroughly enjoys recording each wedding in a spontaneous and natural way – people feel comfortable when they're in front of Steve's camera – producing classic and contemporary images for stylish couples who value fine photography.

Steve is passionate about people, beauty and ceremony, and inspired by love – the love couples have for each other, the love for them by their families, and the gathering of all of their loved ones to witness their marriage. Steve has been happily married for over thirty years, has two beautiful daughters, and understands the importance of family.

Name: Laura Sparling
Company Name: Beads by Laura
Website: www.beadsbylaura.co.uk

Laura has been making beads since 2004. She saw an advert in the back pages of an American beadwork magazine that showed equipment for making your own glass beads. Having always been a creative person who had tried pretty much every craft going, she'd been experimenting with making jewellery since childhood but hadn't realised it was possible to actually make glass beads at home. She bought some books and researched the subject for many weeks, eventually putting together a very basic lampworking kit. She set herself up in the back garden with her dad's trusty old Black & Decker Workmate and Horace, her Hot Head Torch (which provides an intense flame used to melt the glass). They eventually converted the garden shed into a pleasant bead-making space. She upgraded her single-fuel torch to a dual-fuel set-up and has worked with it ever since.

Beads by Laura was born when she started selling her beads on eBay and then she would buy new glass with the proceeds. This was before Etsy and easy-to-build websites existed. For a couple of years, lampworking was her hobby and her way of relaxing after work.

When Laura started making beads, she and her parents were running a small print-finishing and mailing business in Southampton, and she was also managing a company selling bespoke, hand-made Christmas and wedding crackers. Sadly, her mum died suddenly in 2006 and Laura and her dad decided to call it a day with the business; neither of them could bear the thought of carrying it on without her. So Laura decided to try to support herself by making beads and teaching lampwork, and her hobby became her job.

In 2010, Laura moved to Cambridge to be with her husband, Chris.

Name:	Kelly Swallow
Company Name:	Kelly Swallow
Website:	www.kellyswallow.com

Kelly Swallow is an Irish designer now based in Hertfordshire. A lifetime of sewing, designing and creating, coupled with a passion for fabrics, led her to set up her upholstery design business in 2009.

Kelly creates fabulous individual and bespoke pieces of furniture. Capturing a little piece of history, she sources antique items and reinvents them with a patchwork of exquisite fabrics with personality and meaning. She designs and creates using unusual and surprising combinations of vintage and treasured fabrics. Each piece of patchwork is meticulously crafted to reflect and enhance the character of each individually sourced piece of furniture.

At the start of her career, she spent many years working for Greenpeace before starting her business and there is a strong ethical thread running through her work. Every chair frame that she uses is effectively up-cycled. She also now has many contacts who are textile designers who generate high-quality waste fabrics, some of which can be used in her designs.

Kelly often undertakes commissions for special occasions like weddings, anniversaries or birthdays. The client can have input throughout the process, sometimes incorporating their own treasured textiles or embroidered pieces so that the finished piece truly weaves their story in fabric, creating an heirloom for the future.

Kelly's chairs have been used in *Masterchef, DIY SOS, Sky Sports Rugby Club* and TV adverts and are regularly featured in interiors, craft and lifestyle magazines.

Kelly sells ready-made pieces and also undertakes commissions via her website or through independent shops and galleries. Kelly has a loyal international customer base.

Name:	Richard Weston
Company Name(s):	Weston Earth Images Ltd;
	Richard Weston Studio Ltd
Website(s):	www.westonearthimages.com;
	www.richardwestonstudio.com

Richard Weston is an architect, designer and author. After graduating with a first-class Honours degree in architecture from Manchester University, he won the Thouron Award to study Landscape Architecture at the University of Pennsylvania. During thirty years as a university teacher, latterly as Professor of Architecture at Cardiff University, he became a well-known author of acclaimed books and articles on architecture and design, and was Editor of *Architectural Research Quarterly*.

As a designer, Richard has won national competitions and exhibited several times at the Royal Academy of Arts' Summer Exhibition.

In 2003, he began capturing digital 'data from nature', and this led, seven years later, to his being discovered as a scarf designer by Liberty of London. Weston scarves, based on data captured from minerals, are now sold internationally in high-end department stores and boutiques. Their development was featured on the BBC series *Britain's Next Big Thing*, and in magazines globally. Weston Earth Images Limited is now managed by Martin and Helen Price.

In 2013, Richard retired early from full-time academic work to focus on his multi-disciplinary practice, and teaching as a visiting professor. His fascination with 'data from nature' is now being pursued with a sophisticated optical microscope, and applications include a three-storey 'agate façade' for a house in Camden by Patel Taylor Architects, which won the *Sunday Times*'s award for Small House of the Year in 2012.

Richard works on self-generated projects and creates high-resolution digital images for innovative surface design applications in architecture, urban spaces and gardens. He is also working on CreateForAll, a suite of creative and educational apps intended to enable anyone, from children to adults, to participate in the digital revolution as creative producers, not just passive consumers.

Index

accounts 161
  apps 161
  SAGE accounting system
    161
advertising 129, 137–8
  online 129
  print advertising 129, 137–8
  rate cards 137
  series of ads 137–8
advertorials 129–30
agents 110
Alger, Paul 43, 66–7
apprentices 176
apps
  accounts 161
  pricing 107
art *see* Bromley, Dominic and
  Frances; Goodenough,
  Rosemary; Gregory, Celia
  Persephone; Hart, Celia
authenticity 134
awards i, 136, 141, 157–8

Barakat, Shima ix–xii

bead-making business *see*
  Sparling, Laura
bespoke services 51–2, 77
'big idea' *see* product idea
Birtles, Martha 155
blogging 67, 70, 73
board of directors 154, 155
bookkeeping 18, 170
brand building 39
brand communication 37
British Hallmarking Council i
brochures 171
Bromley, Dominic and Frances
  12–13, 19–20, 44–6, 88,
  149, 186–7
Brymer Jones, Keith 10–11,
  28–9, 67, 80–1, 96, 100, 118,
  163–4, 194
business advice 149–59
  asking for advice 150–1
  author's experiences 150–1,
    152, 155–8
  board of directors 154, 155
  business consultants 151–2